SCIENCE IN OUR WORLD

THE EARTH
in SPACE

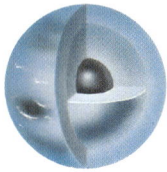

Contributory Author
Brian Knapp, BSc, PhD
Special Illustrations
*David Hardy, Vice President for Western Europe,
International Association of Astronomical Arts*
Art Director
Duncan McCrae, BSc
Special scientific models
*Tim Fulford, MA, Head of Design and Technology,
Leighton Park School*
Editorial consultant
Rita Owen, BSc
Special photography
Ian Gledhill
Science advisor
*Jack Brettle, BSc, PhD,
Chief Research Scientist, Pilkington plc*
Print consultants
Landmark Production Consultants Ltd
Printed and bound in Hong Kong
Produced by
EARTHSCAPE EDITIONS

First published in the United Kingdom in 1993
by Atlantic Europe Publishing Company Limited,
86 Peppard Road, Sonning Common, Reading,
Berkshire, RG4 9RP, UK
Telephone 0734 723751; Fax 0734 724488

Publication Data
Knapp, Brian
    The Earth in space – (Science in our world; 22)
    1. Astronomy – For children
    2. Earth – For children
    I. Title   II. Series
525
            ISBN 1-869860-87-X

In this book you will find some words that have been shown in **bold** type. There is a full explanation of each of these words on pages 46 and 47.

Experiments that you might like to try for yourself have been put in a yellow box like this.

Acknowledgements
The publishers would like to thank the following:
Leighton Park School, Stephen Samuels and David Woodroffe.

Picture credits
t=top b=bottom l=left r=right
All illustrations are from the Earthscape Editions library except
the following: David Hardy 6/7, 28/29, 43 inset.
All photographs are from the Earthscape Editions library except
the following: ESA/Starland Picture Library 10l, 15b; ESO/Starland
Picture Library 27b, 42/43, 45tl; Michael Pace/FAS/Starland Picture
Library 18bl; NASA 13tr, 14t, 14b, 15tl, 30l; National Optical
Astronomy Observatories/Starland Picture Library 21br, 27t, 32bl, 40;
NROA/AUI/Starland Picture Library 26; University of Dundee 15tr.

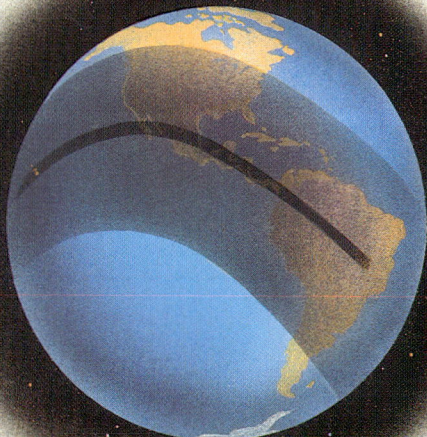

Contents

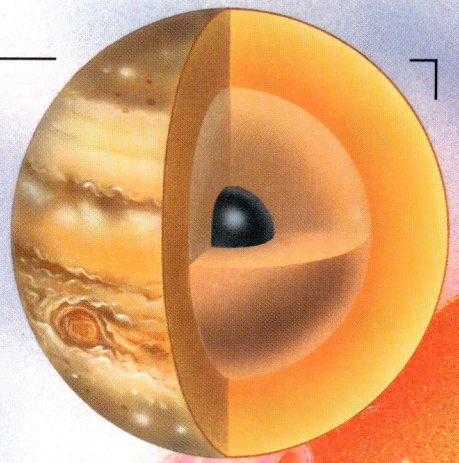

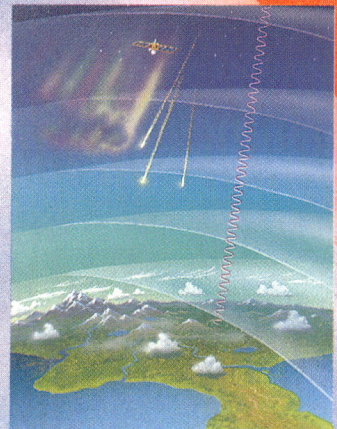

Introduction

eclipses
page 20

asteroids
page 38

tides
page 22

galaxies
page 42

Moon
page 30

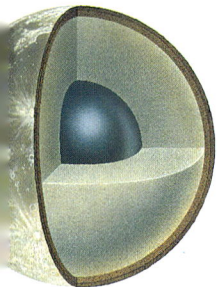

Sun
page 32

Look out of the window and see the Sun shining brightly. The light you see has taken just over eight minutes to travel the 150 million kilometres (km) from our Sun that lies at the centre of the **Solar System**. Look at the sky at night and see the twinkling stars. Each one hints of other solar systems unbelievably far away, each perhaps with their own planetary worlds that still largely remain mysteries to us.

On the scale of the **Universe**, which contains all matter whether formed into stars, planets or just the thin wisps of dust that lie scattered everywhere, the Earth is an insignificant speck. But even this vastness of space and time has rules which everything, no matter how big or how small, must obey. For example, if you drop this book the effect of **gravity** will bring it crashing to the ground following the natural laws that work just as surely and constantly in our world as they do in places throughout the Universe. Switch on a flashlight

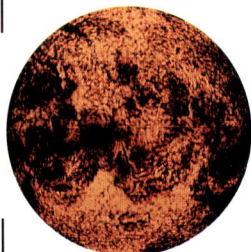

orrery
page 16

rocky planets
page 34

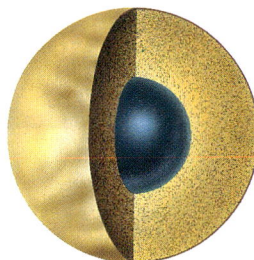

viewing the Earth
page 14

the Solar System
page 6

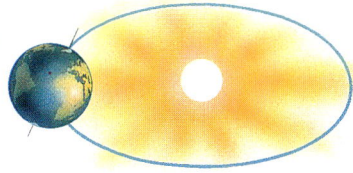

climate
page 24

solar wind
page 12

Earth
page 8

atmosphere
page 10

and the beam of light shoots across a room at just the same speed here as it does everywhere else.

The way the Earth holds the Moon in **orbit** around our planet, how the Moon in its turn produces our tides, and how we get our sunlight and the energy for life are all the result of the Earth's position in space. In turn, the amount of sunlight depends on violent reactions deep inside the Sun, and these in their turn are the result of the way the Universe was formed billions of years ago when the first stars appeared soon after the **Big Bang**.

We may think we live a long way from any influences from space, but the regular appearance of flashes of light – shooting stars – in the night sky demonstrates just how closely we are bound up with the space beyond our **atmosphere**.

Find out about the Earth in space in any way you choose. Just turn to a page to begin your discoveries.

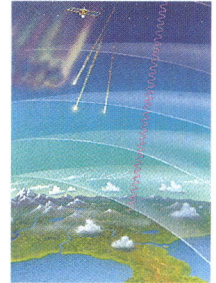

life of stars
page 44

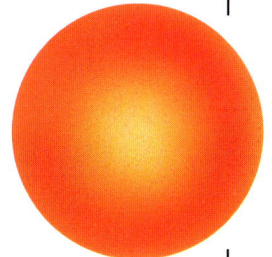

comets
page 40

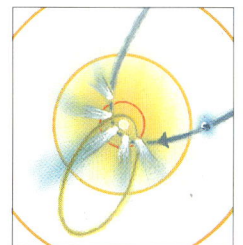

outer planets
page 36

Moon's phases
page 18

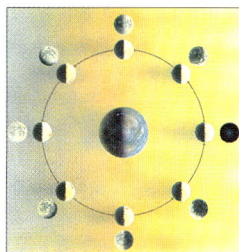

Moon's surface
page 28

telescopes
page 26

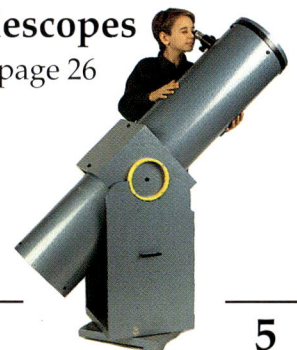

The Solar System

Our Solar System contains nine main orbiting worlds called planets, some with their own moons, orbiting the Sun. They lie far apart from each other, orbiting in different ways and at different speeds, and they spin on their **axes** at different rates. The inner planets including Earth are rocky worlds, whereas the outer planets including the giants of Jupiter and Saturn are mainly made of gases and liquids. Yet despite their differences, each planet is held in place by the gravity of the Sun.

The origin of the Solar System
It is thought that the whole Solar System was formed from a huge cloud of gas and dust made up mostly of the **atoms** hydrogen and helium. The Sun is about three-quarters hydrogen and a quarter helium, and thought to be similar to the original gas cloud. By contrast, the planets are mostly made of atoms such as iron, oxygen and silicon that once existed in the cloud of dust. This makes them very different from the Sun.

(For more information on gravity see the book Falling (Gravity) *in the Science in our world series.)*

Pluto

Neptune

Uranus

The size of the Solar System
The enormity of the Solar System can be judged by the time a particle of light (a **photon**) leaving the Sun and travelling at about one billion km an hour (hr) will take to reach each planet. It reaches the nearest planet, Mercury, in just three minutes (min), flies past the Earth after eight minutes, and takes five and a half hours to reach the outermost planet, Pluto, from where the Sun will appear as just a rather brighter disc of light set in the black starry sky.

Saturn

Jupiter

Mars

EARTH

Venus

Mercury

Sun

The Earth as a planet

As far as we can tell, the Earth is unique, an accidental mixture of materials that came together in a very special way some 4.6 billion years ago. At first it was nothing more than a dense mass of gas, but the force of gravity gradually caused the Earth's materials to collapse inwards, heating the core as they did so. The hot core still drives our world.

1 The earliest Earth collected as a mass of gas which collapsed under the force of gravity. **Nuclear reactions** inside this material released further heat and caused the core to become molten.

2 After a billion years the surface had cooled and developed a crust of solid rocks. At the same time the surface was bombarded with **meteorites** that made huge craters just like those seen on the Moon today. Hot rock inside the Earth was continually turned over, dragging the crust apart and allowing vast sheets of molten rock (lava) to flow out and cool to make more crust. This process is still happening today.

3 As the crust thickened and less lava flowed to the surface there was an opportunity for some gases to condense and form the water of the oceans and the atmosphere.

4 Life forms probably developed first in the hot liquids near to volcanic eruptions. Slowly the developing plant life helped to absorb carbon dioxide and release oxygen, changing the composition of the air and allowing life to colonise the land.

North Pole

Equator

23.5°

The Earth spins on an axis which is a line drawn between the North Pole and the South Pole. On average the axis is 23.5° (degrees) to the plane in which the Earth orbits the Sun, but it varies over time (see page 24).

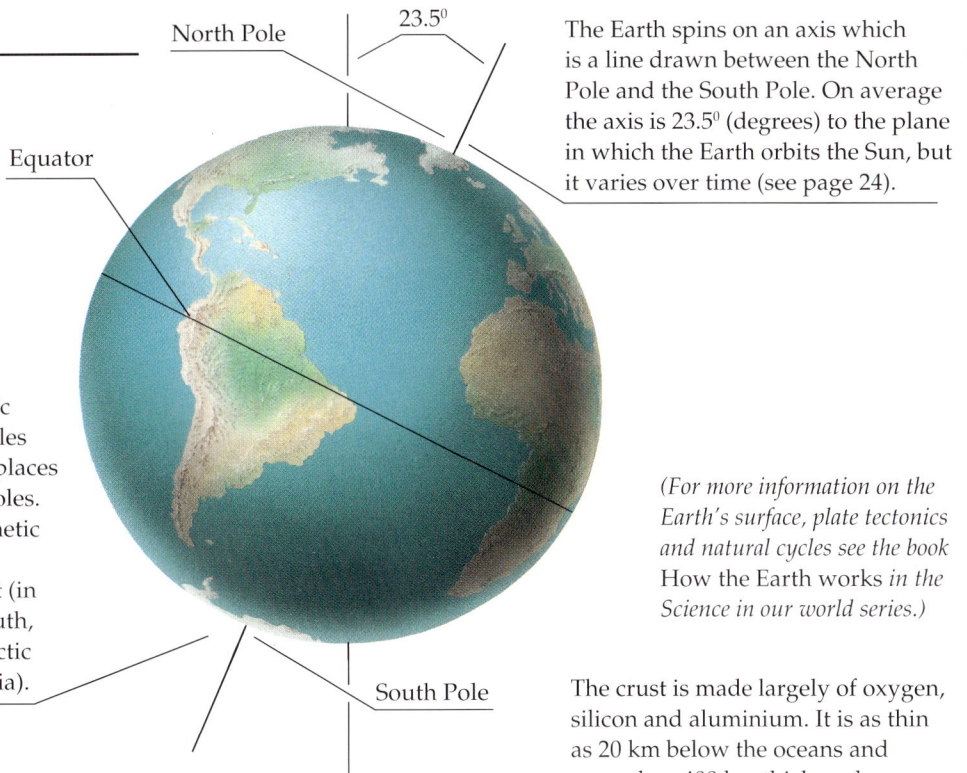

The Earth's magnetic North and South Poles are not in the same places as the geographic poles. At present the magnetic poles are at about 76° North, 100° West (in Canada) and 66° South, 139° East (the Antarctic coast facing Australia).

(For more information on the Earth's surface, plate tectonics and natural cycles see the book How the Earth works *in the Science in our world series.)*

South Pole

Earth: diameter 12,800 km

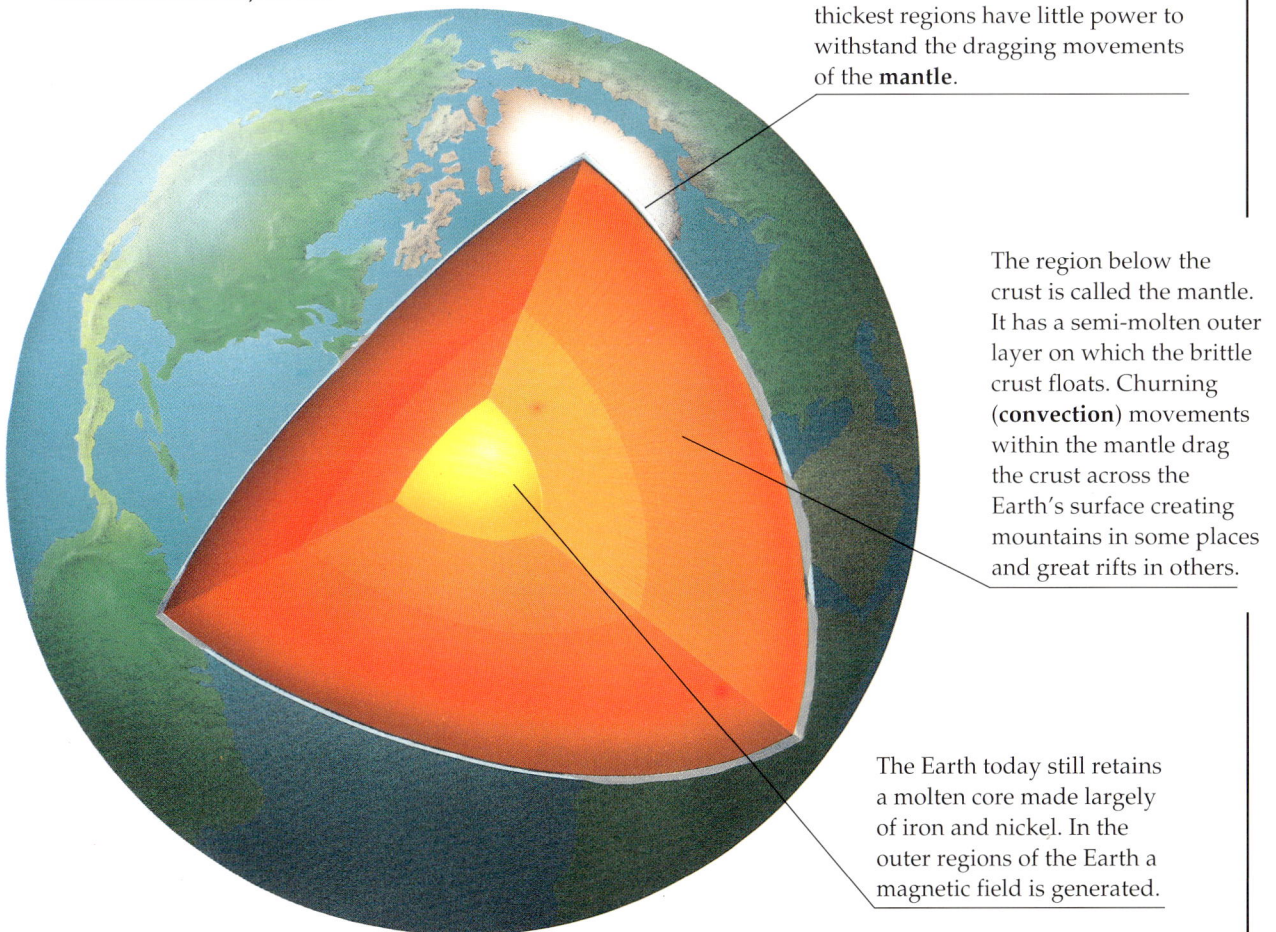

The crust is made largely of oxygen, silicon and aluminium. It is as thin as 20 km below the oceans and more than 400 km thick under some mountains. Nevertheless, even the thickest regions have little power to withstand the dragging movements of the **mantle**.

The region below the crust is called the mantle. It has a semi-molten outer layer on which the brittle crust floats. Churning (**convection**) movements within the mantle drag the crust across the Earth's surface creating mountains in some places and great rifts in others.

The Earth today still retains a molten core made largely of iron and nickel. In the outer regions of the Earth a magnetic field is generated.

The atmosphere

Surrounding the Earth is an invisible 'envelope' of gases known as the atmosphere. Over time these gases have become sorted into layers, each with a different name and different properties.

The lowest part of the atmosphere contains the water vapour that helps to make our clouds and keep our world warm. Above this are layers containing a gas called ozone which shields us from the harmful ultra-violet rays in space. Further out still, there are layers that allow us to send radio waves around the world.

Exosphere (above 600 km from the Earth's surface). Air molecules are very rare at these levels and helium is the most common gas.

Thermosphere (about 500 km thick). Extremely thin air. Readily absorbs ultra-violet radiation. Within this layer lies the ionosphere, the place which bounces back medium (MW) and short (SW) radio waves, allowing them to reach large distances round the world.

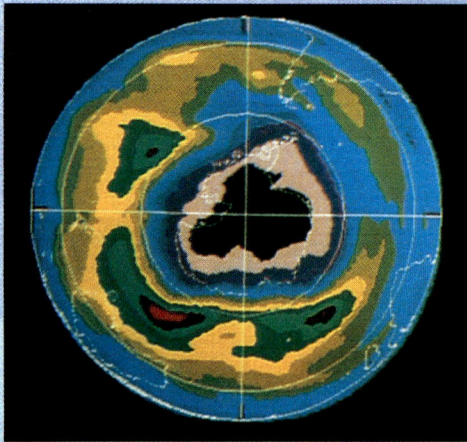

This picture has been generated by a computer from satellite information. It shows the amount of ozone in the atmosphere over the South Pole. Places with a red colour have only small amounts of ozone because of destruction by human-made pollutants.

Mesosphere (about 50 km thick). Transparent to the Sun's rays. Temperature decreases with height.

Stratosphere (about 30 km thick). The air is very 'thin' but contains important ozone gas. Temperature increases with height.

Composition of the atmosphere
The main components of the atmosphere are nitrogen (78%) and oxygen (21%). Other important gases are carbon dioxide and water vapour, although together they make up less than 1% of the atmosphere.

Troposphere (10 – 20 km thick). The layer which contains the clouds. It is mainly transparent to the Sun's rays. The temperature decreases with height.

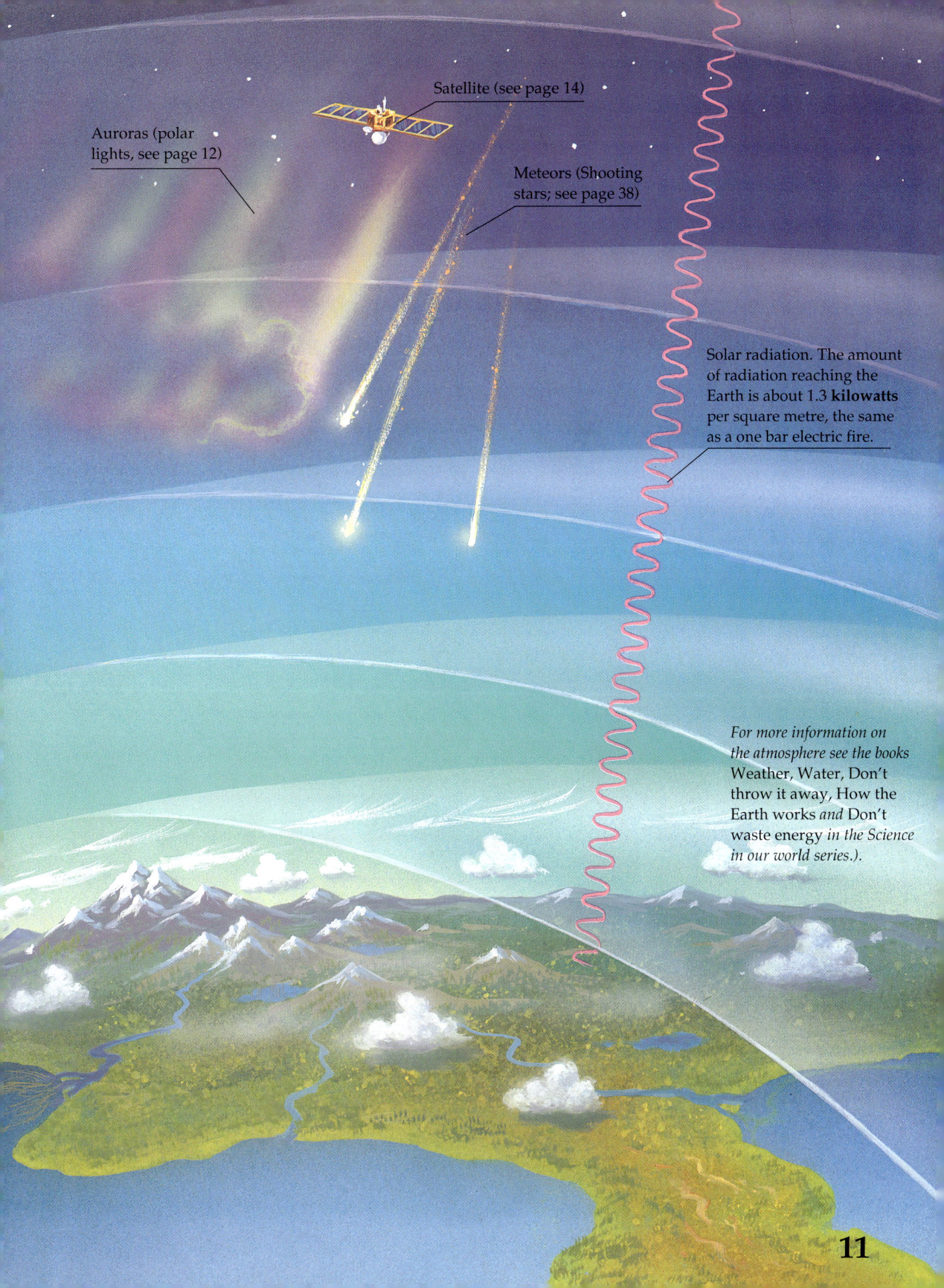

Satellite (see page 14)

Auroras (polar lights, see page 12)

Meteors (Shooting stars; see page 38)

Solar radiation. The amount of radiation reaching the Earth is about 1.3 **kilowatts** per square metre, the same as a one bar electric fire.

For more information on the atmosphere see the books Weather, Water, Don't throw it away, How the Earth works *and* Don't waste energy *in the Science in our world series.).*

11

Beyond the atmosphere

The Sun is continuously sending out a stream of particles into space. As they move through space they create the solar wind. The Earth is always in the path of the solar wind, and the outer layers of the atmosphere are constantly being caught by it.

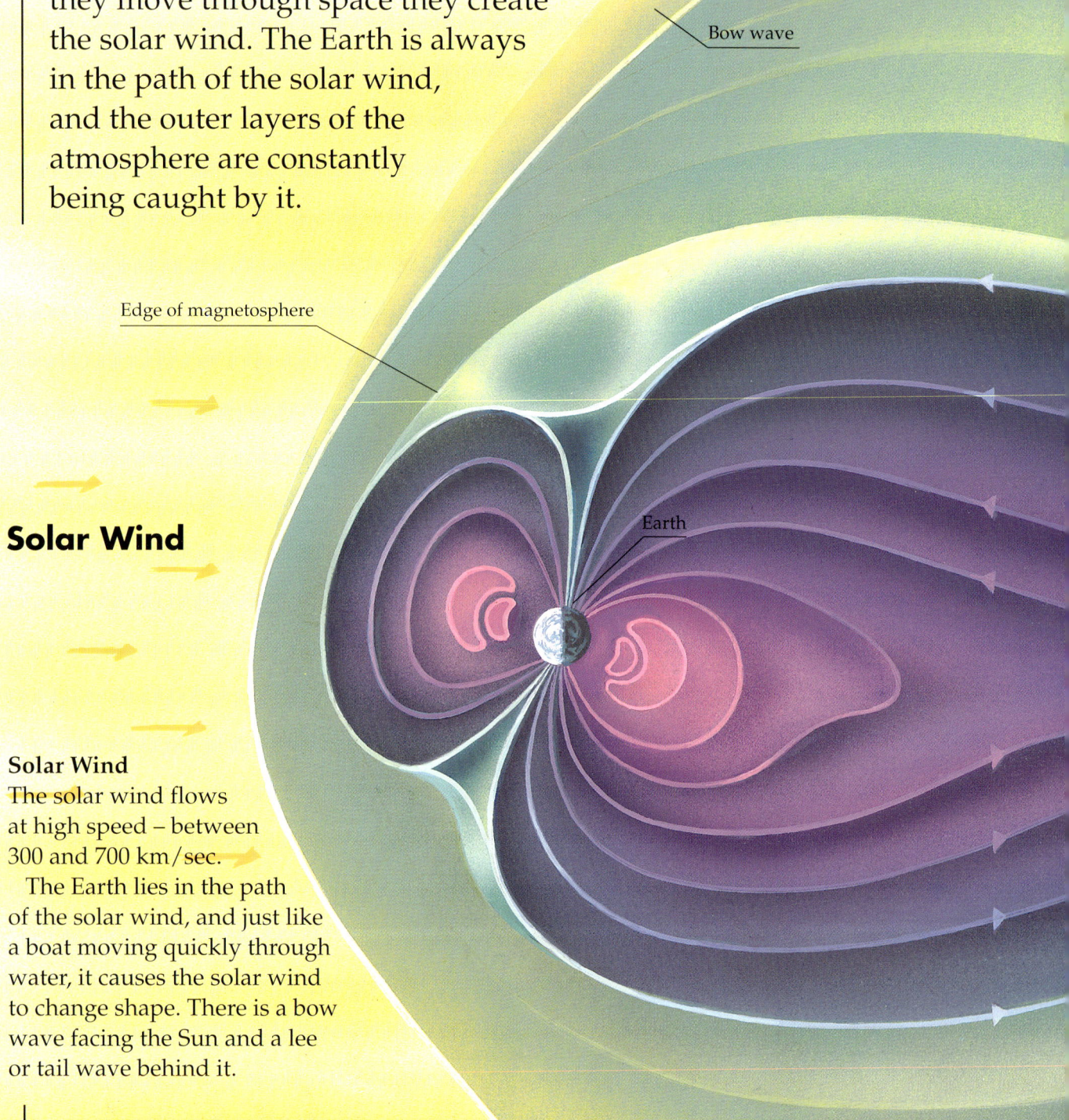

Bow wave

Edge of magnetosphere

Solar Wind

Earth

Solar Wind
The solar wind flows at high speed – between 300 and 700 km/sec.
  The Earth lies in the path of the solar wind, and just like a boat moving quickly through water, it causes the solar wind to change shape. There is a bow wave facing the Sun and a lee or tail wave behind it.

The auroras

People who live near to the North and South Poles can sometimes see a phenomenon called an aurora. This is created by the solar wind beating against the magnetosphere. Colours are produced when energy from the magnetosphere is channelled into the upper atmosphere of the Earth where it sets off a reaction and causes the air to glow. The green colour is made by charged oxygen gas, the crimson colour by charged nitrogen gas.

This is the aurora borealis, the northern lights seen from a spacecraft. The brightness of the auroras depends on sunspot activity (see page 32).

Tail of magnetosphere

The magnetosphere

This is a giant invisible shell beyond the Earth's atmosphere. It reaches about ten Earth diameters forward of the Earth and several thousand Earth diameters back into space, forming a tail. The magnetosphere does not contain any air from the Earth, but it is where the magnetism from the Earth reaches out into the solar wind. The power produced in this region is about 100 billion watts, and part of the power is used in making the night-time displays called auroras.

Views of the Earth

The Earth's surface has many patterns that are impossible to see from the ground or even from an aircraft. However, satellites orbit the Earth just far enough away to see detail and yet show the broad patterns of the Earth's surface.

The Earth has no natural light of its own. Its colour comes from the reflected light of the Sun. Nearly three-quarters of our planet is covered by water. This is why the Earth looks blue when seen from space.

LANDSAT is a satellite that records the way plants, rocks and water send out, or radiate, heat waves into space. Red in this image tells of green meadows, the blue grey areas on land are bare rock and the white areas are snow-covered mountains. This image of the part of Iceland near the capital Reykjavik was taken from an altitude of just over 900 km.

Viewing the land

One of the most important groups of satellites are those designed to look at the Earth's surface. One of these satellites (known as LANDSAT) scans the surface and shows not just the shape of the land, but also the distribution of healthy and diseased vegetation, where the sea is polluted and much more.

In a few sweeps around the Earth, LANDSAT images reveal detail of the surface that would be impossible to provide from the ground. LANDSAT is especially valuable for surveying inaccessible areas and in the search for fuels and minerals buried beneath the surface.

An orbiting satellite. In the background you can see the size of view that a satellite can cover.

The picture below shows a part of North West Europe taken by a polar orbiting satellite. The patches of cloud streaming across most of the land are called cumulus clouds. The larger the clouds, the more the chance of rain. Such pictures are important for short-term weather forecasting.

(For more information on the Earth's weather see the book Weather *in the Science in our world series.)*

Weather eye

Satellites can show what changes are occurring in the patterns of clouds. There are two types of satellite. One kind takes a broad view. It remains over the same place above the Earth (a geostationary satellite) and shows the cloud patterns over most of one hemisphere. The other kind of satellite orbits the poles. It is called a polar-orbiting satellite. The polar-orbiting satellites travel much closer to the Earth's surface than the stationary satellites and give details for accurate weather forecasts.

This picture was taken from a geostationary satellite situated over Africa. The patches of white near the Equator are thunderstorm clouds; large swirling masses of thick white cloud near the poles belong to weather systems called depressions.

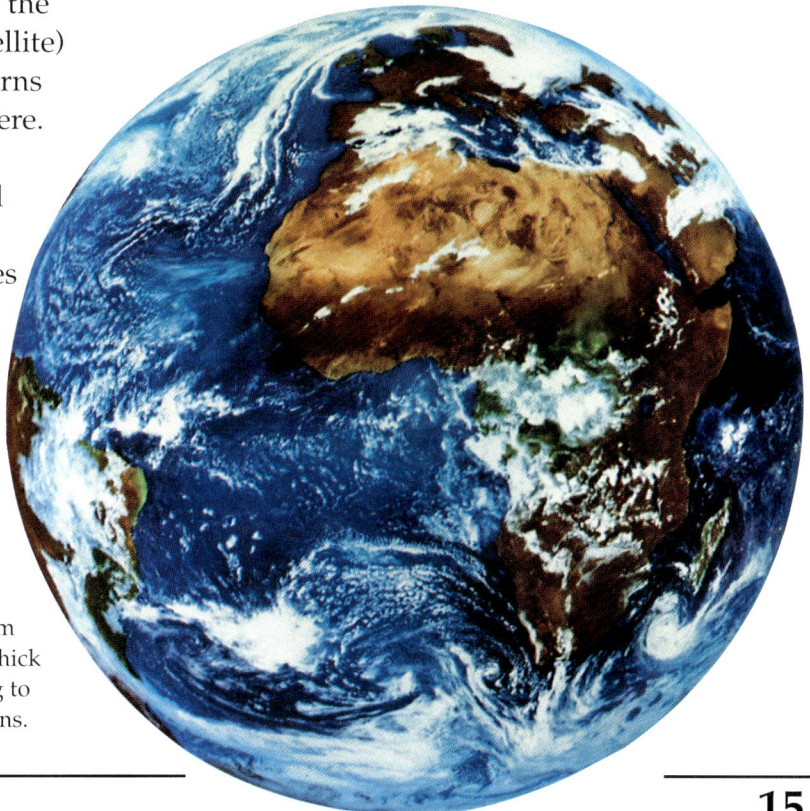

Modelling Sun, Moon and Earth

An orrery is a model invented centuries ago to help people understand the way the Sun and the planets move through space. The model can be made to include all the planets and you may be able to see one in your local museum. In this self-build example many simplifications have been made, but it will still help you to investigate many things about the Sun, Earth and Moon, including the nature of eclipses and tides.

Investigate the movement of the Earth and Moon
The sizes of Sun, Earth and Moon in an orrery are, of course, not true to scale. The model, however, does show the principle of how the Earth spins, and by using the bulb and a darkened room you can imagine the phases of the Moon as seen from the Earth and you can experience the eclipses. Remember that the Moon always keeps the same side facing the Earth, so it can be connected to the Earth with a fixed wire.

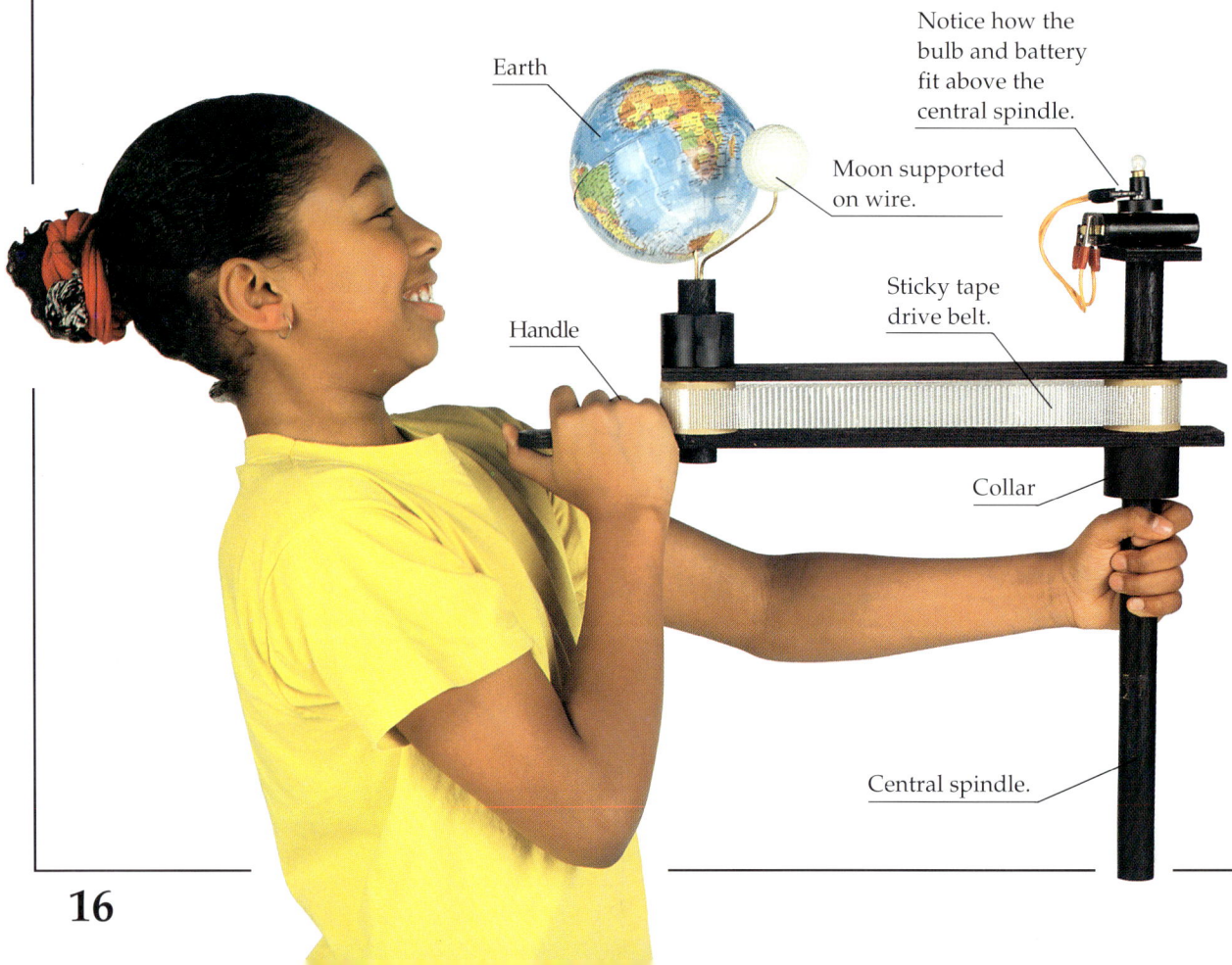

Earth

Notice how the bulb and battery fit above the central spindle.

Moon supported on wire.

Handle

Sticky tape drive belt.

Collar

Central spindle.

The orrery: components

Wire to connect electrical equipment

Bulb

Golf ball (Moon)

Model Earth from toyshop

Clips to connect bulb to battery

Battery

Arm to support the Earth is fixed into the dowel rod together with the Moon support.

Stiff wire to support the Moon

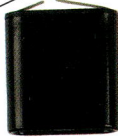

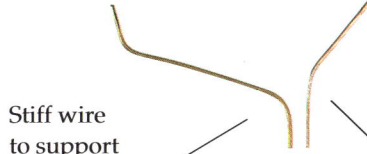

Baseboard for battery attaches to top of central spindle.

Collar glued to outer spindle.

Outer spindle

Arms made from plywood with holes for spindles.

Sandpaper strip

These collars have a sandpaper strip glued on the outside.

Collars of cardboard or plastic tubing

The lower arm can be given a handle of your own design to help with ease of rotation.

Central spindle

Use a strong sticky tape as the drive belt.

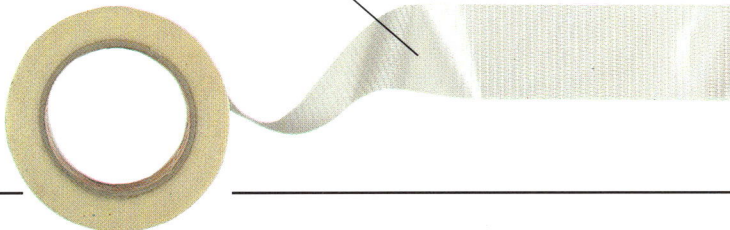

An eclipse of the Sun as modelled by the orrery.

Phases of the Moon

Neither the Earth nor the Moon have any light of their own, but, as they orbit the Sun they are illuminated by light from it. The way we see this illumination gives the phases of the Moon.

The lunar month
The Moon revolves around the Earth in 27 days, 7 hr, 43 min and 11.6 sec. This is called a sidereal month. However, because the Earth is also moving around the Sun, the time it takes for the Moon to make a complete orbit and return to the same phase (i.e. have the same illumination when seen from the Earth) is a little longer – 29 days, 12 hr, 44 min and 2.8 sec.

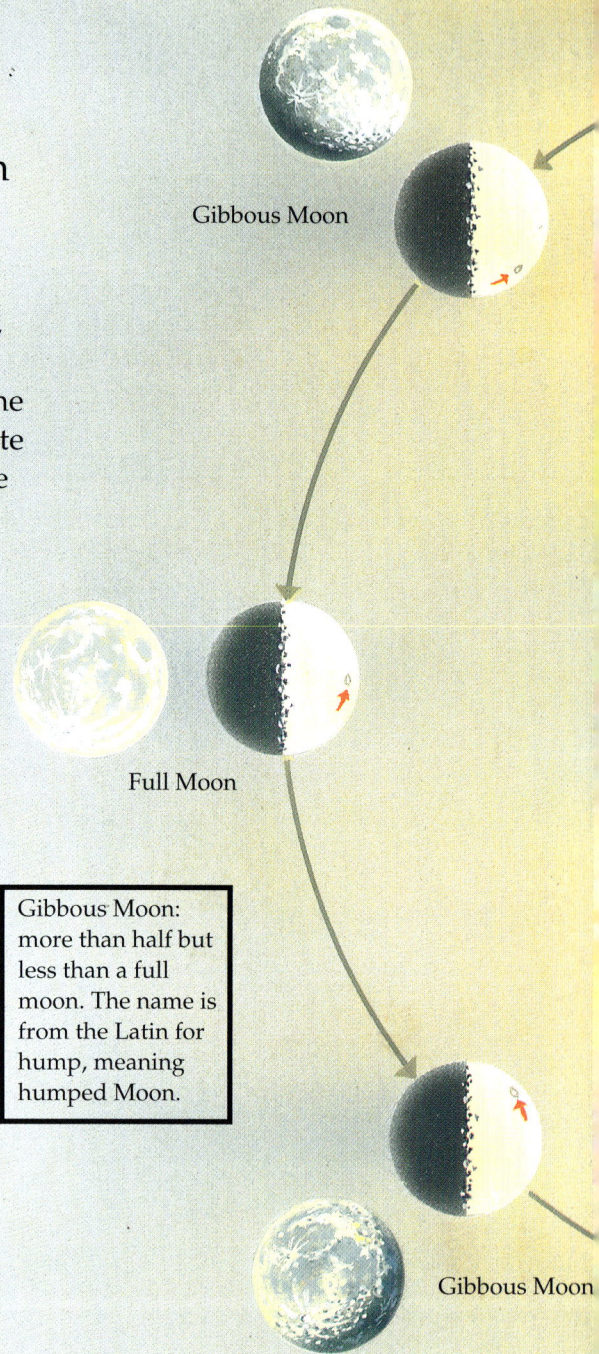

Gibbous Moon

Full Moon

Gibbous Moon: more than half but less than a full moon. The name is from the Latin for hump, meaning humped Moon.

Gibbous Moon

The photograph on the left is of a crescent Moon.

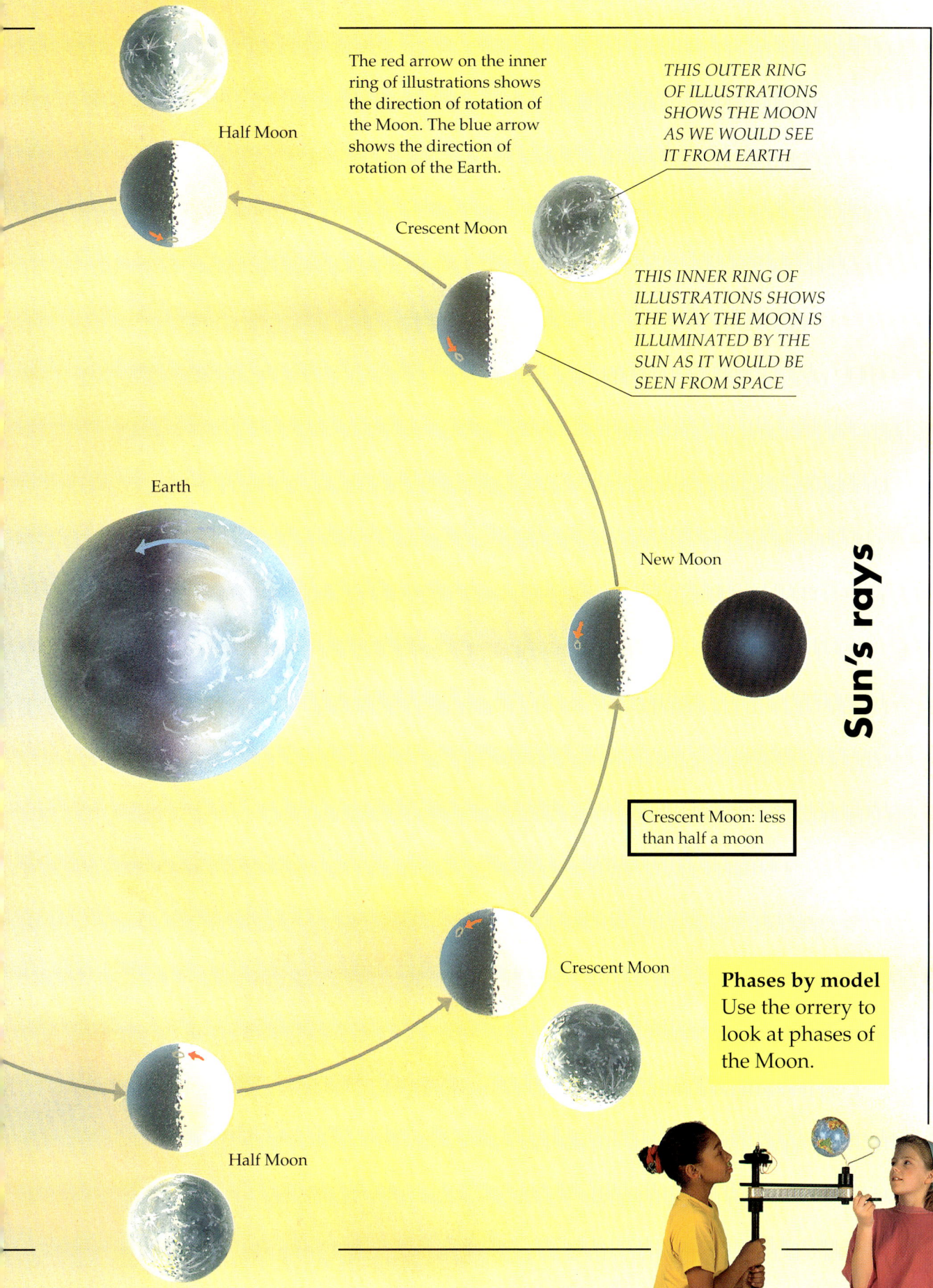

Half Moon

The red arrow on the inner ring of illustrations shows the direction of rotation of the Moon. The blue arrow shows the direction of rotation of the Earth.

THIS OUTER RING OF ILLUSTRATIONS SHOWS THE MOON AS WE WOULD SEE IT FROM EARTH

Crescent Moon

THIS INNER RING OF ILLUSTRATIONS SHOWS THE WAY THE MOON IS ILLUMINATED BY THE SUN AS IT WOULD BE SEEN FROM SPACE

Earth

New Moon

Sun's rays

Crescent Moon: less than half a moon

Crescent Moon

Phases by model
Use the orrery to look at phases of the Moon.

Half Moon

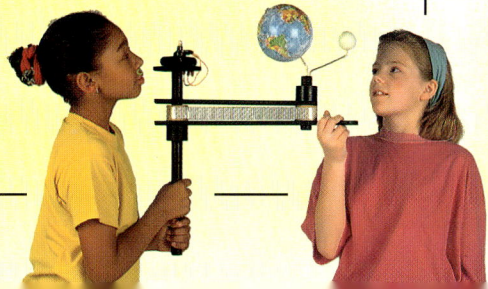

Eclipses

An eclipse occurs when the normal sunlight received by the Earth or the Moon is blocked because the paths of the Moon and Earth cross. Sometimes the Earth blocks out light reaching the Moon, giving an eclipse of the Moon; more spectacularly, the Moon blocks out light reaching the Earth, giving an eclipse of the Sun.

During an eclipse only a small band of the Earth (at most 270 km across) experiences total darkness (called an umbra). But for people in this small band, the sky suddenly darkens and stars become visible. A much larger band of the Earth's surface experiences partial darkness (called the penumbra); here people still see a milky white sky.

This picture shows the path traced by the umbra and penumbra during an eclipse.

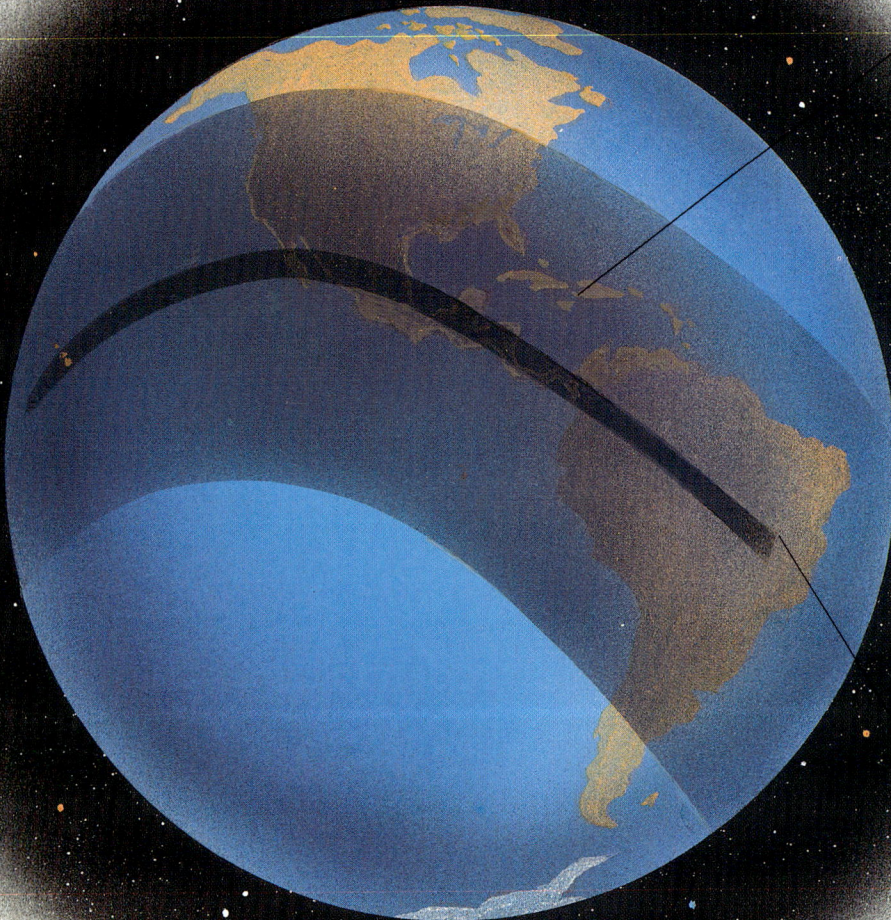

The eclipse lasts for up to seven and a half minutes at any one place.

Two types of eclipse
This diagram shows how the shadow cast by the moon is made up of two parts. The umbra is just a small area of darkness directly behind the Moon; the penumbra (where people see a partial eclipse, i.e. they see only part of the Sun blocked out), is a much larger area as shown by the lighter shading.

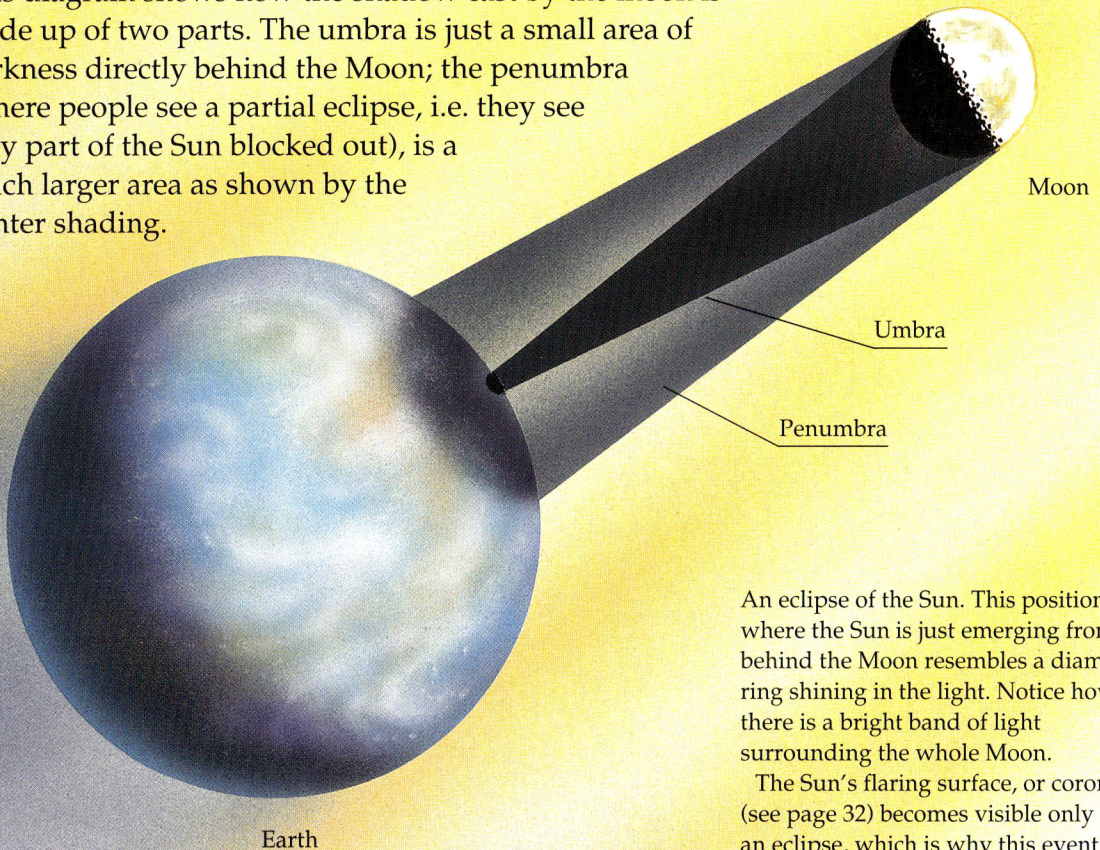

Moon

Umbra

Penumbra

Earth

An eclipse of the Sun. This position, where the Sun is just emerging from behind the Moon resembles a diamond ring shining in the light. Notice how there is a bright band of light surrounding the whole Moon.

The Sun's flaring surface, or corona (see page 32) becomes visible only during an eclipse, which is why this event is so important to scientists studying the Sun.

Make your own eclipse
By placing the orrery in a darkened room, as shown below, you can see the way total and partial eclipses occur.

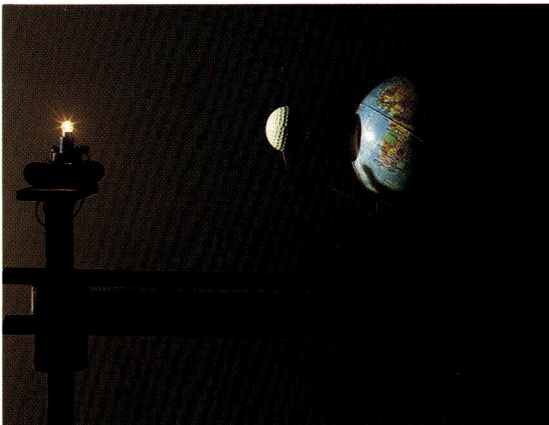

The Earth's tides

There are two high tides (and therefore two low tides) each day. One set is caused by the gravitational pull of the Moon and to a lesser extent by the Sun, and the other by the way the Earth and Moon together orbit the Sun.

Although they have quite different causes, the two high tides occur exactly on the opposing sides of the Earth.

The diagram below shows how the passage of the Moon across an ocean basin draws the ocean waters with it, creating high and low tides.

In practice such things as the complicated shape of the ocean basins cause the high and low tides to move in a circular path around the edge of the ocean basins.

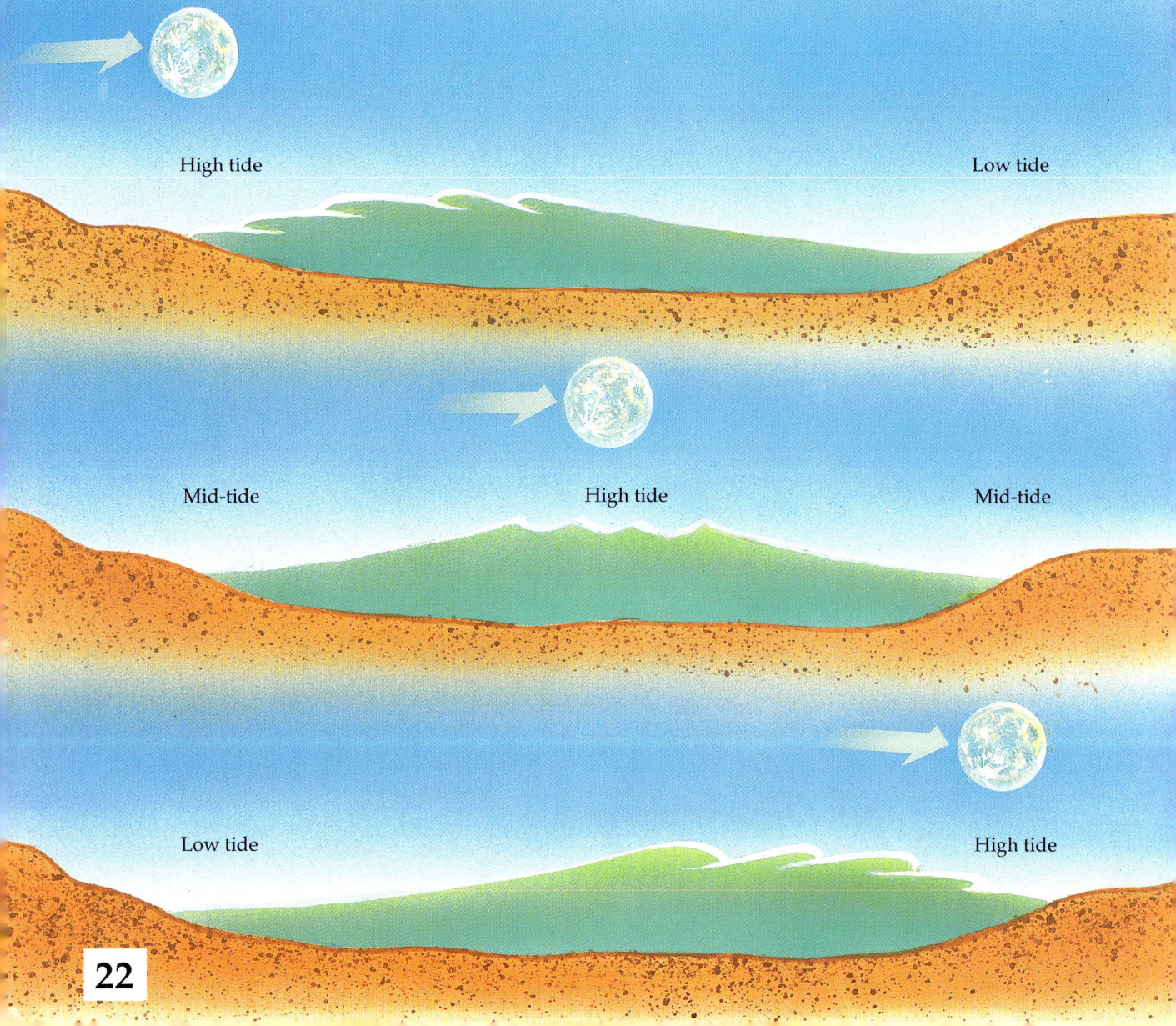

High tide

Low tide

Mid-tide

High tide

Mid-tide

Low tide

High tide

The spinning tide

The Earth and Moon spin round the Sun so fast that, if it were not for the Earth's gravity, the ocean waters would all flow to the side of the Earth which is facing away from the Sun and fly off into space! Although the Earth's gravity holds the ocean waters on the surface, the spinning effect of the Earth is powerful enough to ensure that there is always a high tide on the side of the Earth facing away from the Sun.

The gravity tide

The Moon's gravity pulls the waters of the oceans towards it because it is so close to the Earth. As the Moon orbits the Earth it therefore causes ocean water (and the high tide) to move across the Earth's surface as well, causing regular periods of high and low tide.

The Sun is so far away that it has less effect than the Moon. Often Sun and Moon pull water in different ways, but when they act together they give a high ranging (spring) tide and when they oppose they give a low ranging (neap) tide.

(To find out more about the way a spinning body tends to move outward, see the book Falling (Gravity) *in the Science in our world series.)*

Make tides in an ocean

If you put your hands into a circular bowl of water and then move them across from one side to the other you will cause a high 'tide' to form on one side of the bowl. Take your hands from the water and watch it flow back.

Experiment to see what happens if you make more high tides in a regular way by rocking the bowl. Use some crystals of permanganate of potash to trace the water movements. Does the water simply move back and forth or does a tide begin to move round the bowl as happens in a real ocean?

The Earth's climate and space

Although the weather may change from day to day, we expect that, in the long-term, we will have the same pattern of weather each year. This is called the climate.

The climate determines, for example, which plants will grow in each part of the world, which animals will survive, and how much ice will build up near the poles. But the climate does not stay the same: there have been times, such as during the **Ice Ages** when the climates all over the world have changed; and there are more regular changes as well. Many factors are involved, but the way the Earth moves through space is very important.

This shows the Earth tilted at 21.5^0.

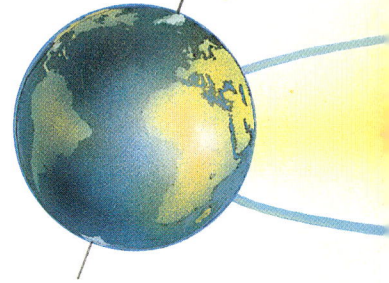

The graph below shows how the Earth's temperature has changed over the last 400,000 years.

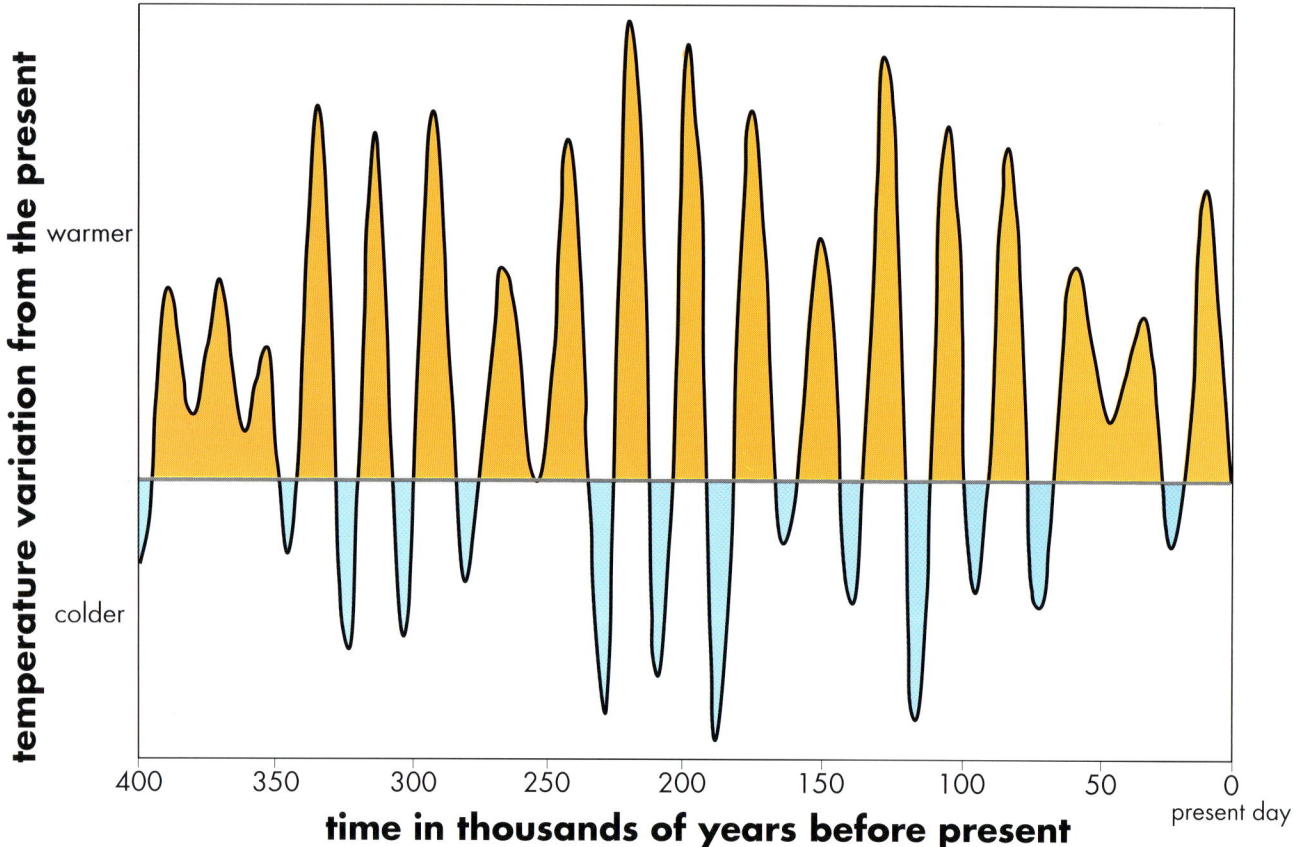

warmer

colder

temperature variation from the present

| 400 | 350 | 300 | 250 | 200 | 150 | 100 | 50 | 0 |

time in thousands of years before present

present day

Elliptical orbit

Circular orbit

This shows the way the Earth
moves when its orbit is an ellipse.

Sun

This shows the
Earth tilted at 24.5^{0}.

Sun

This shows the way the
Earth moves when its
orbit is nearly a circle.

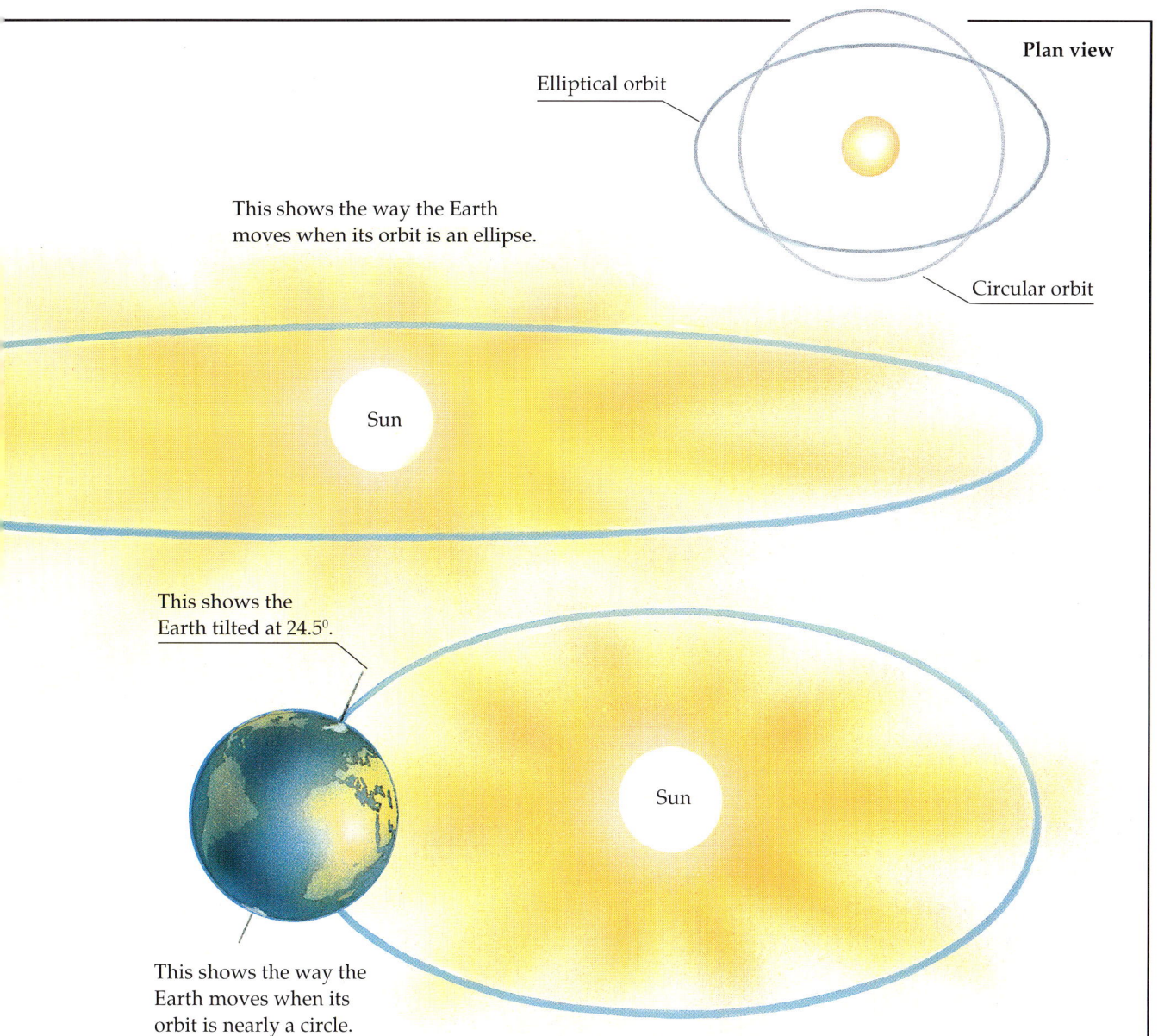

How the Earth moves

The angle at which the Earth is tilted relative to the Sun varies. At the present it
is 21.5 degrees, but over a period of 40,000 years it can become over 3 degrees
larger than this. When the Earth tilts more, there are bigger differences between
seasons; when the Earth tilts less the differences between the seasons are smaller.

The Earth also changes its orbit around the Sun in a regular way. At times it is
almost circular, but over a period of 97,000 years it changes shape until it follows
a path like a giant oval (an ellipse) and then the Earth will be cooler both in
summer and winter.

These ideas about the Earth's changing movements were used by a scientist
named Milankovitch to suggest underlying causes for changes in the Earth's
climate and the start of the Ice Ages.

Looking into space

The Earth is a long way away from even its closest neighbour, the Moon. As a result, with the naked eye you can see very little detail of the Moon and almost nothing of the more distant planets.

The best way for most people to look at any detail on the Moon is to use a pair of binoculars, but when scientists want to look at stars and planets in much greater depth they have to use special telescopes.

Radio telescopes do not have lenses, but gather weak radio signals and focus them at the centre of a concave reflector dish. A computer then analyses the signals received and displays them on a computer screen or prints them on paper. Groups of telescopes (known as arrays of telescopes) can be linked to give the power equivalent to a much larger single telescope.

Optical and radio telescopes
These two types of telescope do not so much compete, as add to the store of knowledge about the Universe. The optical telescope directly captures the weak light sent out by distant stars (and the reflected light from nearby planets). Many stars also transmit energy in addition to visible light and these can be detected using radio telescopes. Maps of the stars produced by radio telescopes show stars that transmit radio waves strongly; star charts produced by optical telescopes show only those that transmit visible light. For this reason, the resulting charts may show many differences.

Optical telescopes at the
Cerro Tololo Inter-American
Observatory, Chile,
South America.

The Milky Way (part of the Galaxy, see page 42)
seen by an optical telescope in an observatory.

(part of the Galaxy, see page 42)

An amateur astronomer looks at the Moon,
planets and distant stars through a 260 mm
reflecting telescope (but never the Sun
because of the danger of focused light to
his eyes!).

The Moon's surface

The Moon, which is a natural satellite of the Earth, appears to be almost trapped in time. Whereas we are used to the surface of the Earth changing, nothing has changed on the Moon for over 800 million years. In this time some of the continents on the Earth's surface have travelled half way round the world!

The near side of the Moon
The Moon's surface is covered with large craters. Many are incredibly old, perhaps over three and a half billion years old. When the meteorites that caused these craters hit the Moon, there was still no life on Earth and oceans were only just forming. The Moon has not changed since.

Moon probes and Moon landings have helped scientists learn about the Moon and its surface. Here are some of the main US and Russian events that have provided valuable information.

2.1.1959, Soviet Luna 1: the first lunar probe passes within 6000 km of the Moon.
31.1.1966, Soviet Luna 9: the first soft landing on the Moon (Ocean of Storms).
20.7.1969, US Apollo 11: the first manned landing on the Moon (by Neil Armstrong and Edwin Aldrin; project cost $25 billion).

The Moon's orbit
The Moon is about one-eightieth the mass of the Earth. The Moon and the Earth move together like a double planet. The Moon is tilted by just over 5 degrees to the plane in which the Earth moves around the Sun. This oval-shaped orbit takes the Moon as far away from the Earth as 407,000 km and brings it as close as 356,000 km.

The Moon and Earth revolve together in such a way that we only see 59% of the Moon's surface: before spacecraft were sent to photograph the 'back' of the Moon in 1959, nobody had any idea what the far side looked like.

Oceanus Procellarum (Ocean of Storms)

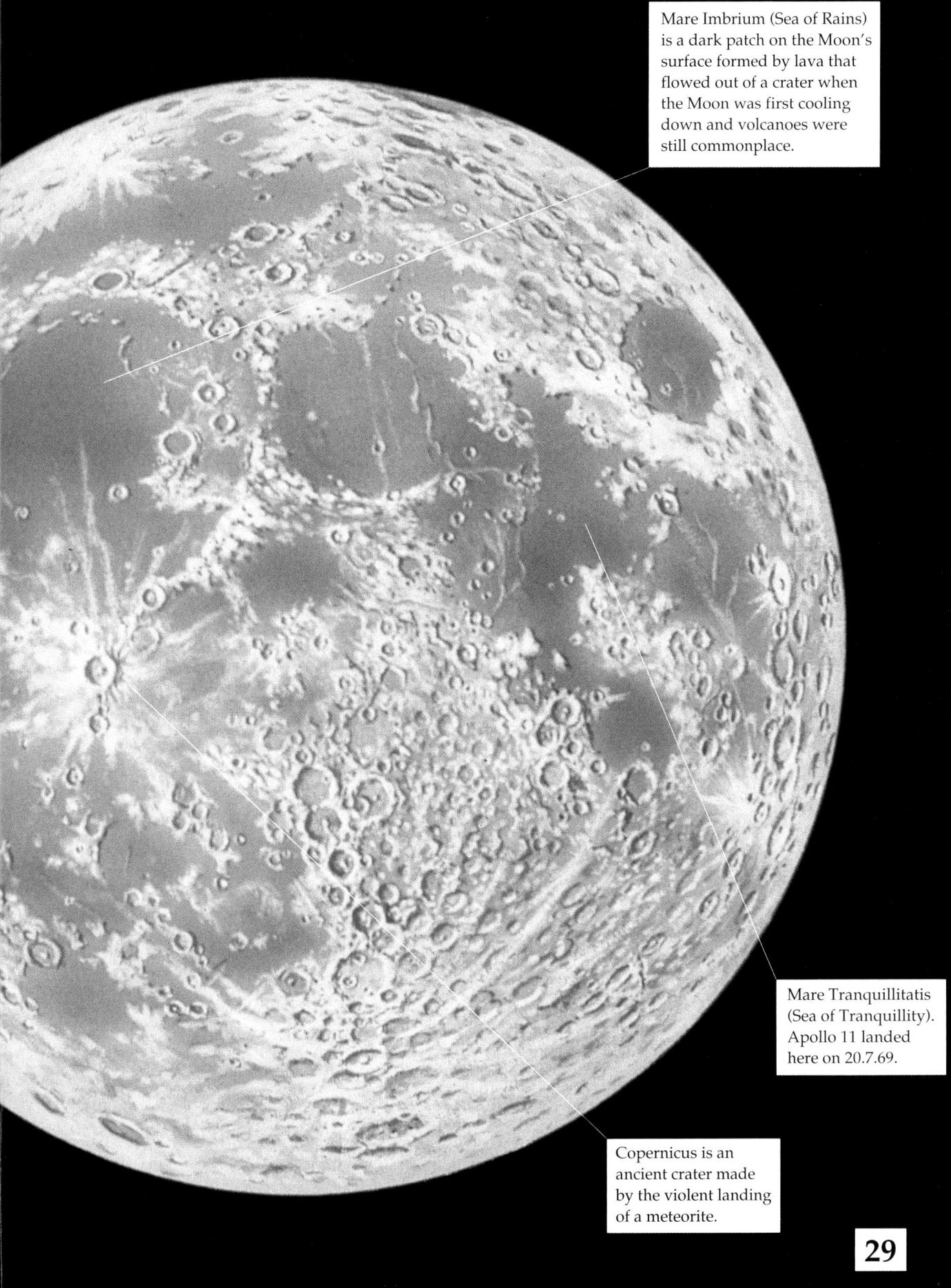

Mare Imbrium (Sea of Rains) is a dark patch on the Moon's surface formed by lava that flowed out of a crater when the Moon was first cooling down and volcanoes were still commonplace.

Mare Tranquillitatis (Sea of Tranquillity). Apollo 11 landed here on 20.7.69.

Copernicus is an ancient crater made by the violent landing of a meteorite.

29

How the Moon was formed

Although there is no life on the Moon, it has a structure made up of layers similar to that of the Earth. The core is, however, hard, which is why the Moon has no magnetic field and which is why the surface never suffers earthquakes. Moreover, there is no atmosphere surrounding the Moon and being much smaller than the Earth, its gravity is less than one-sixth of that on Earth.

Moon   Earth

The surface
There are two types of landscape on the Moon – a rough, bright mountainous land which covers the majority of the surface, and a darker, flatter land which occupies less than a third of the surface. Early astronomers thought of them as 'continents' and 'oceans', which is why the flat areas – even though they are totally dry – are called Seas and Oceans on lunar maps.

The Moon's structure
The Moon's rocks are not unlike some of those found on Earth. During the first half a billion years of the Moon's history it was still hot enough for volcanoes to produce great lava flows. However, since then it has cooled and all activity has died away. As a result there are no overturning movements – the reason the surface has been left undisturbed for so long.

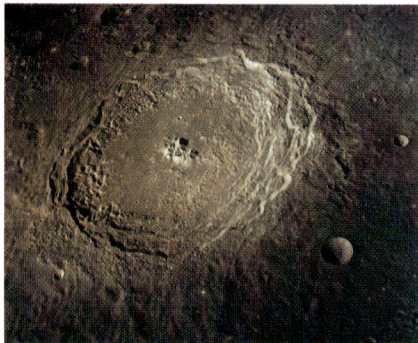

Crater Langrenus is 120 km wide

Formation of a crater: meteoroids drawn towards the Moon by gravity.

Crater

Cratered surface

Craters cover the Moon's surface. The largest (like the Sea of Rains) are over 1000 km across. They were formed in the early history of the Moon, when meteorites or asteroids (see page 38) struck the unprotected surface. The impact of the larger asteroids would have generated so much heat that the rock would have turned molten and flooded over the land, producing a smooth surface.

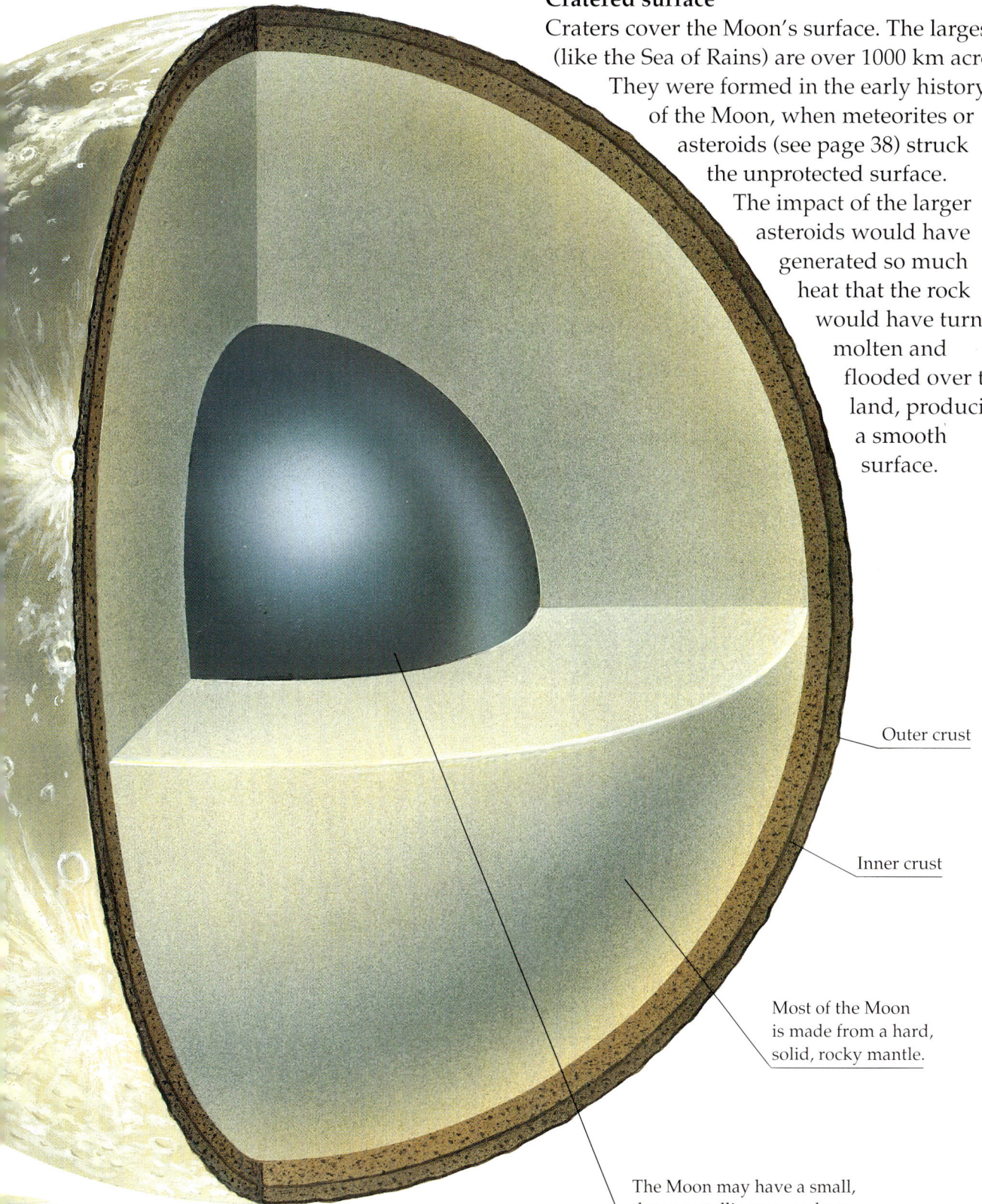

Outer crust

Inner crust

Most of the Moon is made from a hard, solid, rocky mantle.

The Moon may have a small, dense metallic core, perhaps made mainly of iron.

The Sun

The Sun is a star 1.4 million km across whose gases constantly churn over and send huge streams of matter far out into the Universe. We receive just one two millionth of all the energy emitted by the Sun, and yet plants can still capture enough if it to provide the energy for all life on Earth, nearly 150 million km away.

The Sun is so large that it has immense gravitational pull, and can hold all nine of the planets of the Solar System in orbit.

The Sun spins once on its axis every 25 days.

Sunspots (dark) and faculae (light). These show where the Sun is turning over its gases most actively. They last in any one region for between a few weeks and several months. Sunspot activity is linked to the Sun's magnetism and varies in a cycle lasting 22 years.

Prominences and flares. These gigantic solar fireworks are produced when the incredibly powerful magnetic fields of the Sun pull glowing gases away from its surface. They are most common when the sunspot activity is greatest.

Corona. This is the region of thin, intensely hot gases that spread beyond the visible Sun and which is picked out as the faint glow that extends beyond the Sun which can be seen during an eclipse. It is the Sun's version of an atmosphere.

This is an infra-red photograph of the Sun. The darker patches are relatively cool regions.

The yellow colour of the Sun is caused by its temperature. It glows yellow (almost white hot) because its surface is about 6000 $^{\circ}$C.

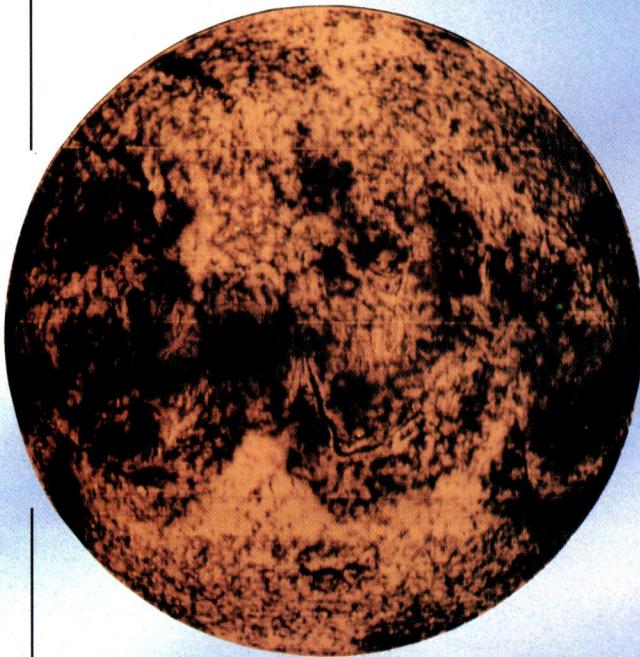

Chromosphere. This is the outer edge of the visible Sun which can be seen shining with a reddish glow during an eclipse. In this region very fine jets of gas shoot out from the Sun at speeds of up to 30,000 km/hr.

Photosphere. This is the visible surface of the Sun, a surface layer of gases where convection cells bubble to the surface.

Radiation zone. Here the gases are so dense that no gas molecules can move. Heat is lost towards the surface by radiation.

Convection zone. This makes up the outer third of the Sun. Here the temperature is 'only' about 1 million degrees Celsius and the gases, turn over and over by convection like a liquid heated in a pan from below. The Sun's gigantic magnetic field is probably formed in this region.

Core. The most dense region of gases have a temperature of about 15 million degrees Celsius. This is the region which acts like a stupendous nuclear power station, and where most of the energy is generated. The energy-making processes have gone on for about five billion years. Scientists believe that within about five billion years time the Sun will have lost enough hydrogen for it to begin to die (see page 44).

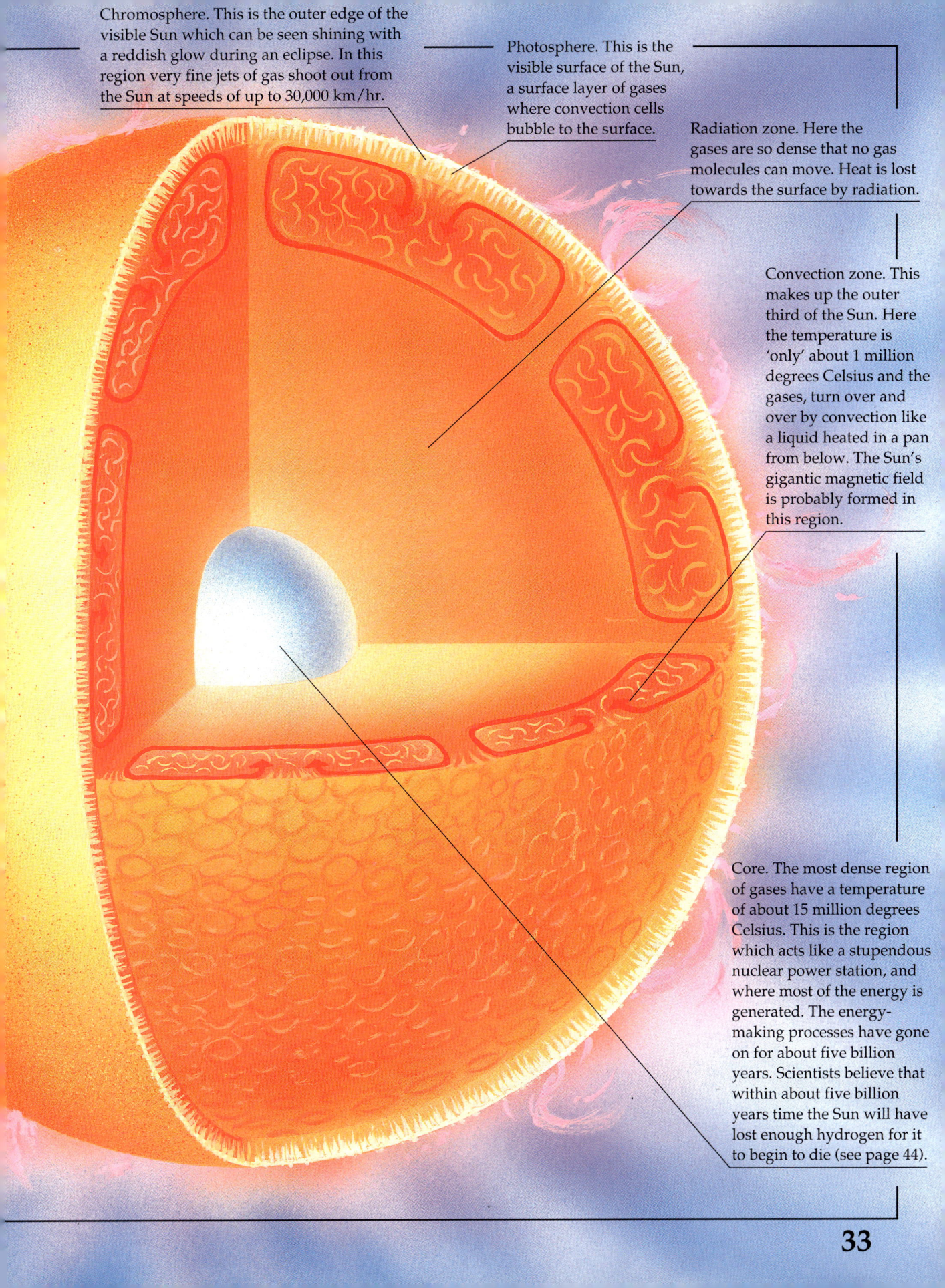

Rocky planets

Although the planets that orbit the Sun are roughly the same age, they vary greatly in their size and the materials from which they are made. The Earth (described on page 8) is one of a group of five planets that are largely made of solid rock. Here are descriptions of the other four.

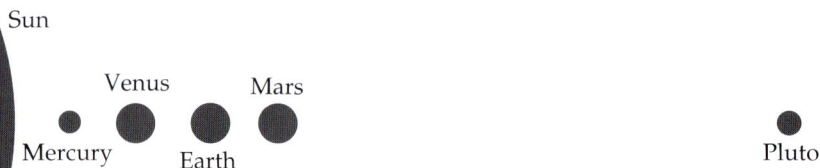

Sun

Mercury

Venus

Earth

Mars

Pluto

Venus: diameter 12,100 km

This planet is the evening and morning 'star' in our skies, and is about the same size as the Earth. However, it is one of the most hostile environments in the Solar System. The shining white 'surface' of the planet is actually an atmosphere with carbon dioxide and sulphur dioxide-rich clouds. From the clouds a rain of sulphuric acid droplets continually falls on the rocky surface.

The atmosphere absorbs heat from the Sun, so that the air temperature is about 480 ^{0}C (a kind of extreme form of the Earth's **Greenhouse Effect**) and it is actually hotter than Mercury, a planet much closer to the Sun.

It is believed there is a molten core similar to the Earth's. Rocks are also similar to those found on the Earth's continents (granite) and below the Earth's oceans (basalt). Venus does not, however, have a magnetic field but it probably did have oceans of water – before the Greenhouse Effect caused them to boil away.

Venus is 108 million km from the Sun, orbiting once every 225 days and spinning on its axis only once every 243 days.

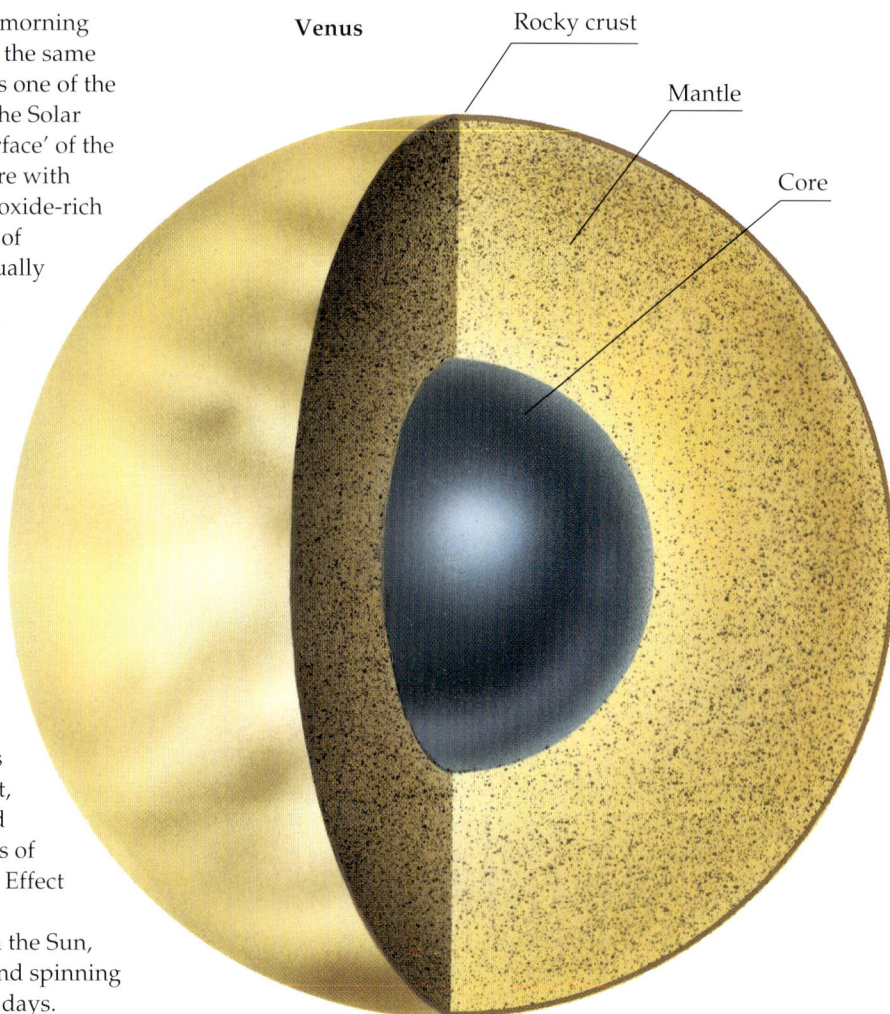

Venus

Rocky crust

Mantle

Core

Mercury

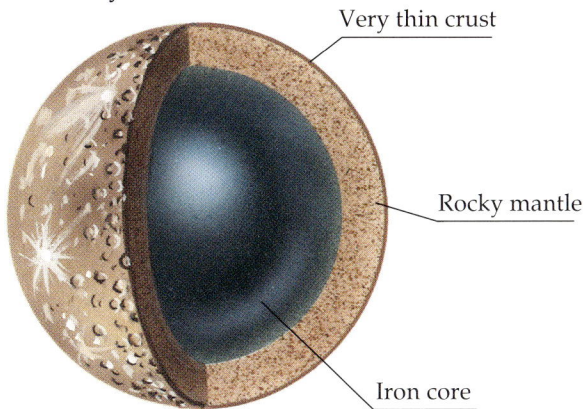

Very thin crust

Rocky mantle

Iron core

Mercury: diameter 4900 km

This planet has a cratered surface similar in appearance to the Moon but it behaves more like the Earth. Mercury is the planet closest to the Sun. This hot world has surface temperatures of 470 °C, nearly five times the boiling point of water.

Mercury is just under half the diameter of the Earth and has a large iron core, possibly molten and responsible for weak magnetic fields. The planet orbits the Sun at about 60 million km once every 88 days and spins on its axis once every 58 days. It has just a trace of atmosphere – mainly made up of sodium, helium and hydrogen.

Mars: diameter 6800 km

About a tenth the mass of the Earth, Mars has a thin atmosphere rich in carbon dioxide. The dry rocky surface is covered with orange sand and is constantly swirled about by driving winds. The sand makes the planet look red when seen in the night sky. Mars has two moons, Phobos and Deimos.

Mars spins on its axis at about the same rate as the Earth and orbits 240 million km from the Sun. Mars appears to have strange features on its surface, called canals, making people wonder if there has ever been life on the planet. Some 'canals' are, in fact, rift valleys, signs of the way the surface formed. Others may well be dried up canyons which were cut by rivers several hundred million years ago. Only ice now exists on Mars.

Volcanoes grow to spectacular heights on Mars: the largest yet spotted – called Mount Olympus – is 24 km high and 500 km across its base, three times the height and four times the breadth of the largest volcano on Earth. Mars has polar ice caps like on Earth, but on Mars they grow and shrink dramatically each year as the seasons change.

Mars

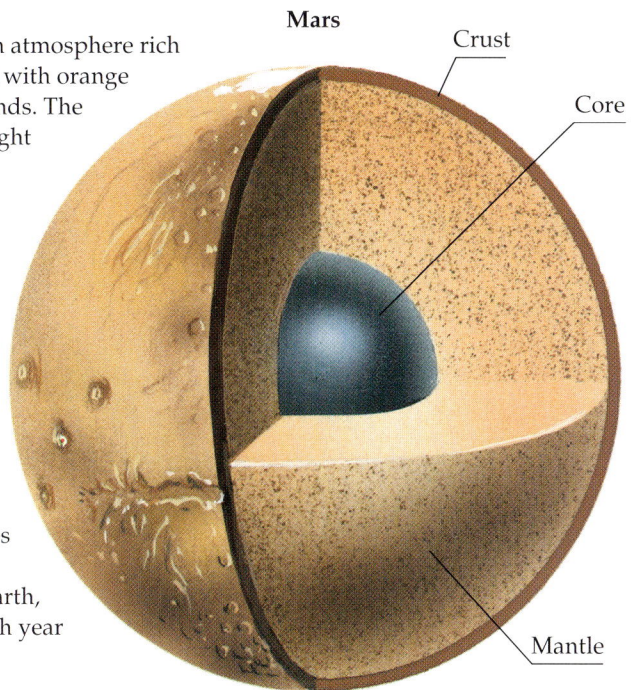

Crust

Core

Mantle

Pluto

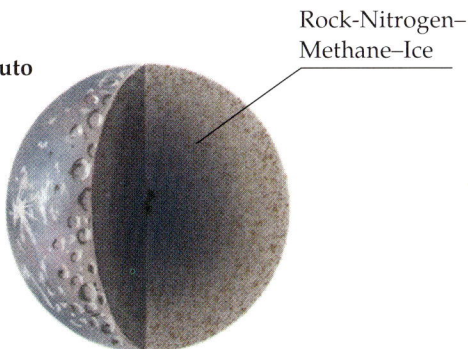

Rock-Nitrogen–
Methane–Ice

Pluto: diameter 2300 km

This is the smallest planet and quite unlike the neighbouring giant planets. Some scientists think it is really no more than a large asteroid. Because of its distance from the Earth and its small size it was not discovered until 1930.

Pluto orbits the Sun once every 248 years at a distance of 5.9 billion km, marking the very edge of the Solar System.

Pluto is a frozen world with an atmosphere of methane gas enveloping a cold rocky core.

Planets of ice and gas

The warmth of the Sun boiled many gases off the surface of the rocky planets. But the outer planets are cold worlds, so far from the Sun that they have never lost their light gases. This is why (except for Pluto described on page 35) they are such giant worlds, made of hydrogen and helium gas or frozen water, methane and ammonia.

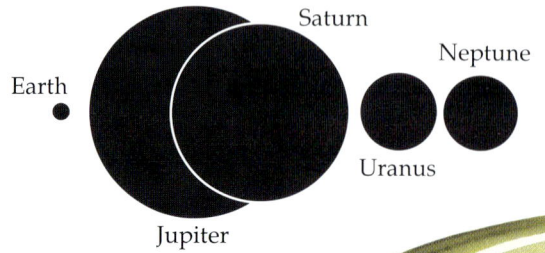

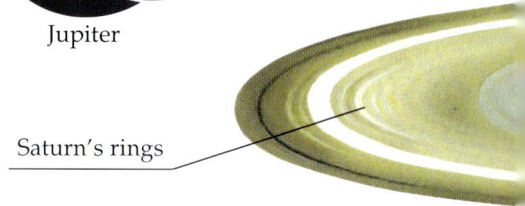

Earth

Saturn

Jupiter

Neptune

Uranus

Saturn's rings

Jupiter: diameter 143,000 km

Jupiter is the planetary giant, over 300 times the mass and a thousand times the volume of the Earth. It is, like the Sun, mainly made of hydrogen and helium. If it were much bigger the gravity of the planet would pull the gases together and turn it into a star. It radiates twice as much heat as it gets from the Sun. Jupiter, some 780 million km from the Sun, rotates once every 10 hr. but orbits the Sun only once every 12 years.

Jupiter began as a small rocky planet two or three times the mass of the Earth. This was enough to hold a huge atmosphere and to compress the gases near the surface into a liquid. Today, therefore, the planet still has a small rocky core, surrounded by thick layers of metallic and liquid hydrogen and helium which merge into an 'atmosphere', also of hydrogen and helium. Jupiter also has an enormously powerful magnetic field.

The atmosphere has winds and clouds that run in streams parallel to the equator; these correspond with the broad coloured bands that can be seen with a telescope.

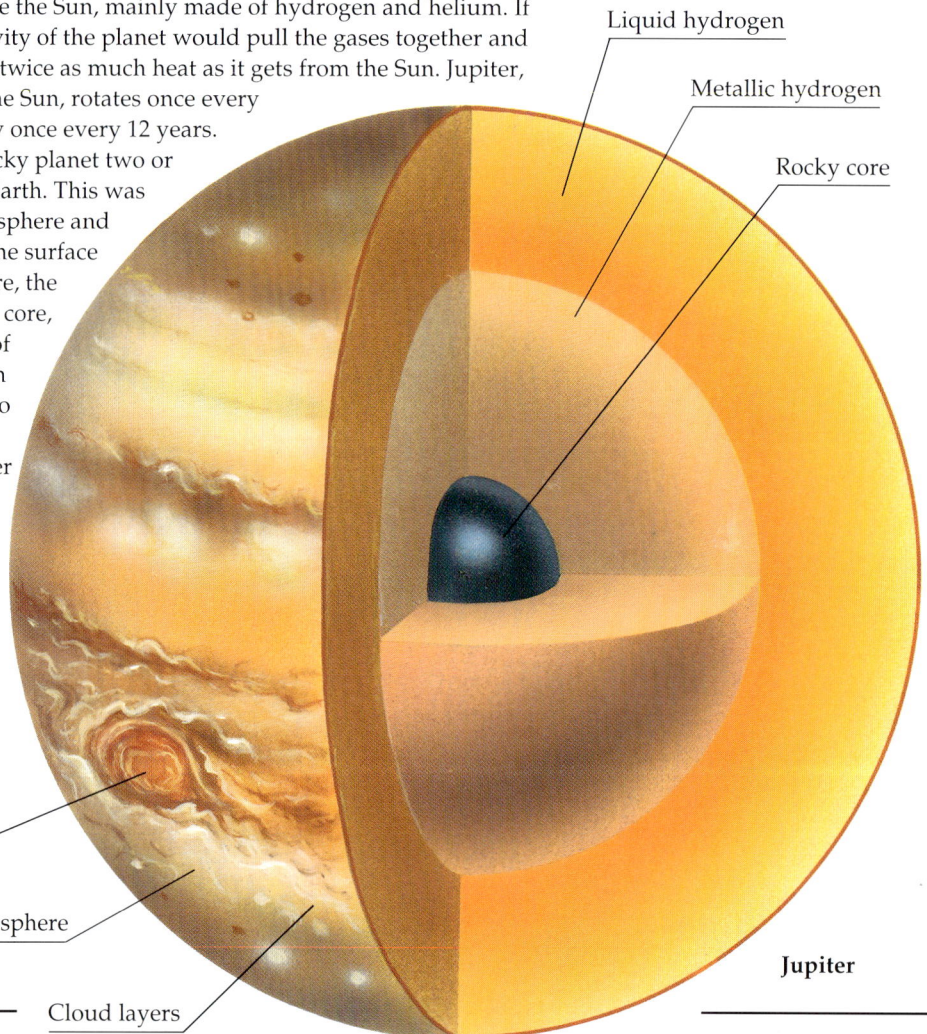

Liquid hydrogen

Metallic hydrogen

Rocky core

Jupiter's spot

Hydrogen/Helium atmosphere

Cloud layers

Jupiter

Saturn

Cloud layers

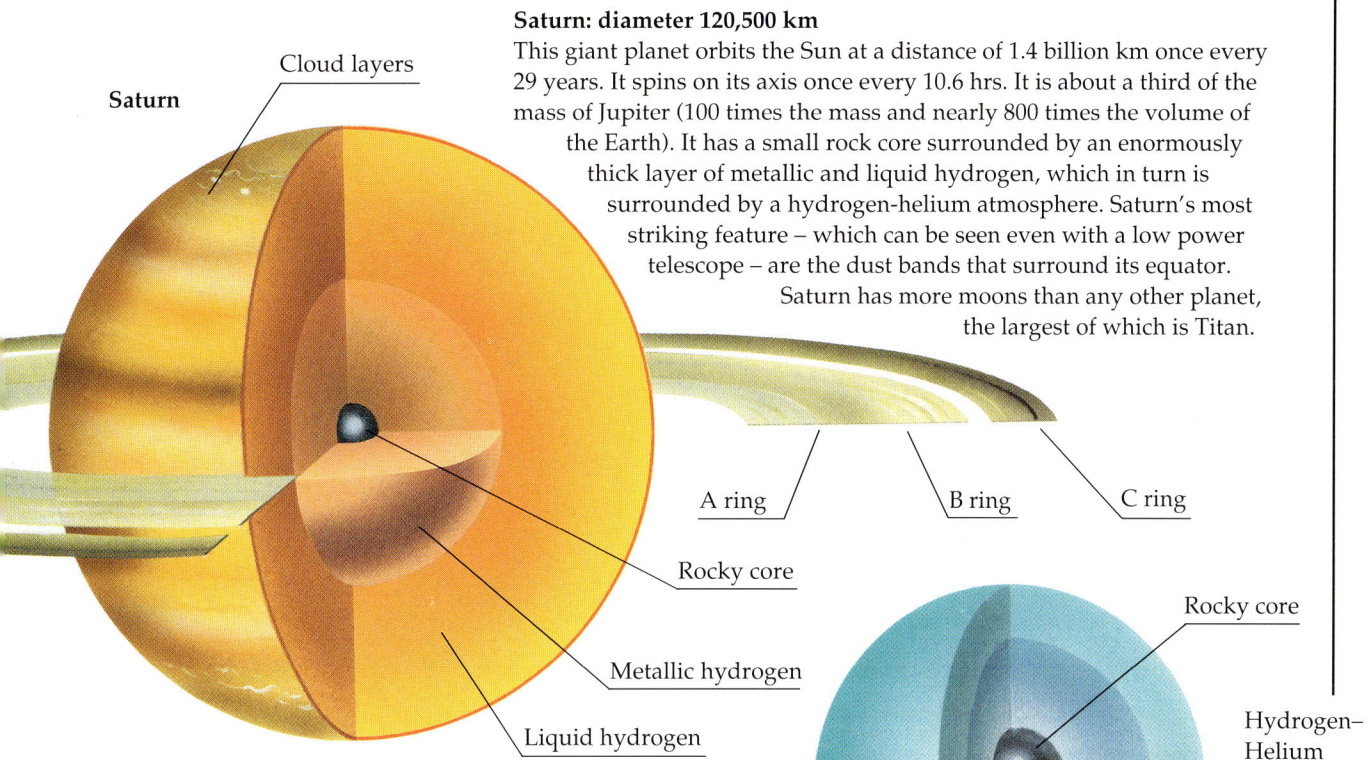

Saturn: diameter 120,500 km

This giant planet orbits the Sun at a distance of 1.4 billion km once every 29 years. It spins on its axis once every 10.6 hrs. It is about a third of the mass of Jupiter (100 times the mass and nearly 800 times the volume of the Earth). It has a small rock core surrounded by an enormously thick layer of metallic and liquid hydrogen, which in turn is surrounded by a hydrogen-helium atmosphere. Saturn's most striking feature – which can be seen even with a low power telescope – are the dust bands that surround its equator. Saturn has more moons than any other planet, the largest of which is Titan.

A ring

B ring

C ring

Rocky core

Metallic hydrogen

Liquid hydrogen

Rocky core

Hydrogen–Helium atmosphere

Moons (Satellites)

Astronomers call any small body that orbits a planet a satellite. The Moon is a very large satellite 'captured' by the Earth. Most other planets have much smaller satellites, or moons. The outer planets have so many moons they are called swarms of satellites. The four largest that orbit Jupiter are each the size of our Moon. The largest moon orbiting Saturn (called Titan) is bigger than the planet Mercury and even has its own atmosphere.

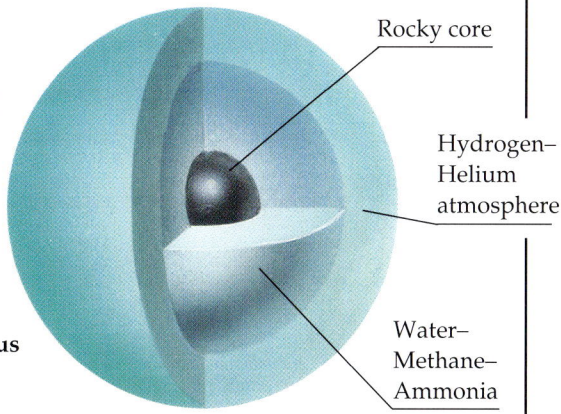

Uranus

Water–Methane–Ammonia

Uranus: diameter 51,100 km

This planet is about four times the diameter and 15 times the mass of the Earth orbiting the Sun every 84 years at a distance of 2.9 billion km. It spins on its axis in just over 17 hrs.

Uranus has an impenetrable atmosphere of hydrogen and helium which is over 8000 km thick. Beneath this is an ocean of hot water over 10,000 km deep. The solid part of the planet is made of rock about the same size as the Earth. At the centre is a core of molten rock. A system of rings surrounds the planet. Uranus also has five major satellites and ten smaller ones.

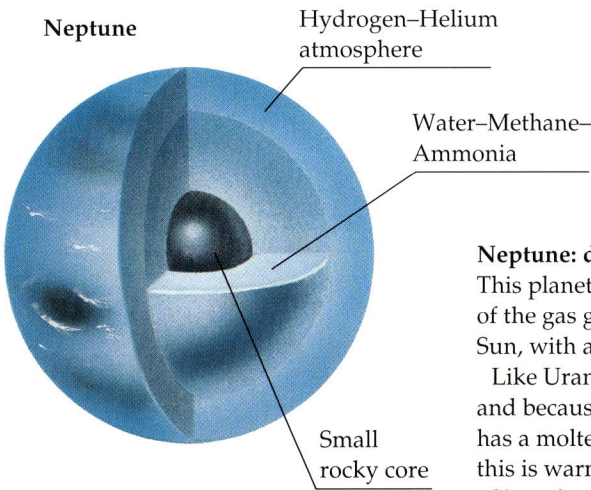

Neptune

Hydrogen–Helium atmosphere

Water–Methane–Ammonia

Small rocky core

Neptune: diameter 49,500 km

This planet is about 17 times the mass of the Earth and the farthest of the gas giants from the Sun, orbiting at 4.4 billion km from the Sun, with a rotation of 165 years and a spin of 16 hrs.

Like Uranus its atmosphere is made of hydrogen and helium and because it has a large magnetic field it is thought the planet has a molten rocky core. The surface is very cold, -220 ^{0}C, yet even this is warmer than would be expected if there was not a source of heat from the core. A system of dust rings surrounds the planet.

Asteroids and meteoroids

There are many rocky fragments in our Solar System that have never been swept together to form planets. Most of the larger ones – called asteroids – swarm in a belt between Mars and Jupiter, although a few have paths that take them near to the Earth; these are known as Apollo asteroids.

Meteoroids are very small rocky bodies, often no more than a few centimetres across. Unlike asteroids they do not orbit the Sun, but seem to be scattered randomly in space. Many are made of mixtures of rock, carbon and water. They cross the orbit of the Earth all the time and can be seen burning up in the Earth's atmosphere at night, making the faint flashes of light called shooting stars. The larger meteoroids can reach the Earth before they burn up completely. The most famous of these formed Meteor Crater in Arizona, USA.

Jupiter

The size and origin of asteroids

The largest asteroid, called Ceres, is over 1000 km across. It is thought that there may be half a million asteroids with diameters bigger than 1 km and countless numbers that are smaller.

Asteroids are most likely fragments from the earliest days of the Solar System. It is probable that many asteroids were once larger, but because they were travelling so close to each other, many must have collided and broken up into the fragments that we see today. Asteroids mostly seem to be made of the same rocky materials that can be found on Earth.

On average a house-sized Apollo asteroid hits the Earth every century; The last one burst over Russia in 1908. An asteroid big enough to threaten life on Earth hits the planet only once every 50 million years or so. The last time this happened may have been the cause of dinosaurs becoming extinct on Earth.

Sun

Mars

For more information on meteoroids, meteorites and craters see the books How the Earth works *and* Falling (Gravity) *in the Science in our world series.)*

Comets

Comets are bodies of ice and rock – like huge dirty snowballs – just a few kilometres across, and yet as they fly through space the solar wind gives them spectacular glowing tails that can reach up to 100 million km in length.

Unlike most planets, which have orbits that are roughly circular, the orbits of comets are very elongated, so that they come very close to the Earth for a short while and then speed off into space and are lost from sight for many years.

Halley's comet

The most famous comet is known as Halley's Comet after the astronomer who predicted the return of one of the most spectacular comets to pass close to the Earth. It has a return cycle of 76 years.

The orbits of comets

Because they are so small, many comets are only detected as they come close to the Earth. About ten new comets are spotted each year, and because each one only returns after many tens of years, this means there must be a large number of them speeding through space. The comet with the shortest orbit is Encke's Comet, which returns every 3.3 years, those with the longest orbits may only return once in several thousand years.

The end of comets

Comets leave a trail of debris behind them as they travel through space. Most of it is made up of tiny pieces of rock, or meteoroids. When the Earth passes through the path of a comet the meteoroids crash into the Earth's atmosphere as meteorites and cause a meteor shower as they burn up in the air.

Halley's Comet photographed as it passed over Chile on 9th January 1986. It has reappeared only 20 times since it was first observed in 239 BC.

This diagram shows the orbits of some comets. Because the orbits of comets cross that of the Earth, comets are among the most likely bodies to collide with the Earth, and some people believe that collisions in the past may have caused widespread destruction, climate change and the extinction of many species. (See also page 38, asteroids.)

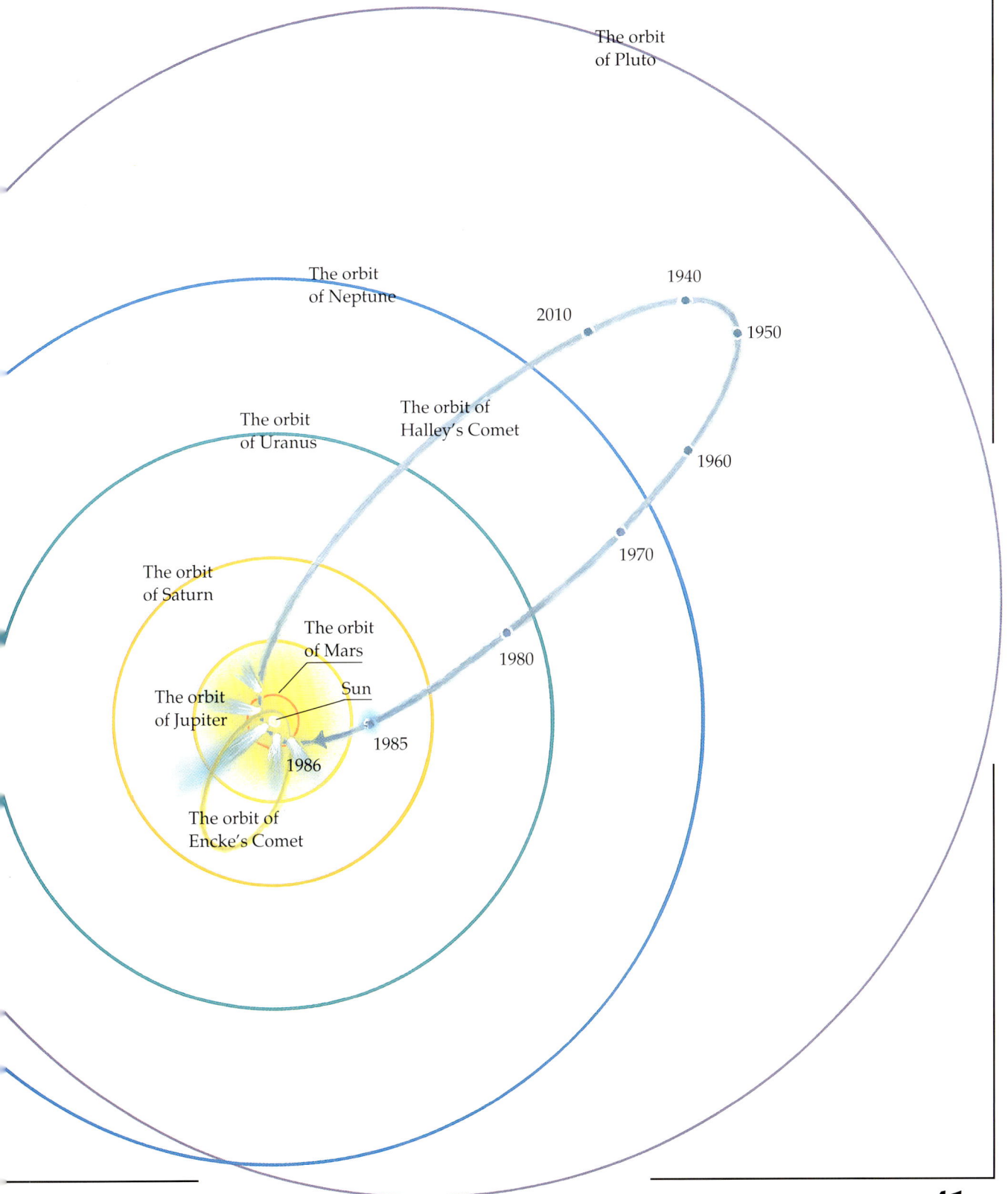

The orbit of Pluto

The orbit of Neptune

1940

2010

1950

The orbit of Uranus

The orbit of Halley's Comet

1960

The orbit of Saturn

1970

The orbit of Mars

Sun

1980

The orbit of Jupiter

1985

1986

The orbit of Encke's Comet

Galaxies

A galaxy is a giant spiral made up of countless stars, gases, dust (and a few planets). We can only see a portion of our galaxy (known as the Galaxy): we call this region the Milky Way. The whole of our galaxy, including the region called the Milky Way, may contain several billion stars, of which our Sun is a tiny member on one of the outer spiral arms.

Set within the Galaxy are stars in many forms of their evolution. Some are new stars set far out on the spiral arms; others, nearer the centre, are up to 15 billion years old; some have even collapsed and produced the strange forms called black holes (see page 44).

This photograph is of the Sombrero Galaxy, a spiral galaxy with a huge nuclear bulge. Around the bulge heavy dust clouds obscure part of the light.

(For more information on light years and on the Big Bang theory of the beginning of the Universe see the book Time *in the Science in our world series.)*

(For more pictures of the Milky Way see the books Time *and* Falling (Gravity) *in the Science in our world series.)*

This picture shows the spiralling arms of the Milky Way region of the Galaxy. The red ring shows the location of the Solar System.

The size of the Galaxy

Our galaxy, like others in the Universe, is disc-shaped. The Galaxy is so big it has to be measured in light years – the distance light travels in one year. The Galaxy is 100,000 light years across and 2000 light years thick. The Sun is over 30,000 light years from the centre of the Galaxy.

Nearby there are 20 large galaxies that together make a cluster. The largest and most prominent of these is called the Andromeda Galaxy, more than 2 million light years away. What we see of this galaxy in the sky is, therefore, what it looked like 2 million years ago!

The life of a star

A star is a large ball of searing hot gas, of which the Sun is a small example. Many stars are millions of km across, although they may only appear as pinpoints of light to us.

Stars may be immensely old, but they are always changing. By looking at many stars, astronomers have been able to piece together the life story of a star. This is what happens.

1 The space between stars contains gas and dust. This can gather into clouds known as nebulae. When enough gas and dust collects in a nebula it quickly collapses into one or more of stars. The gas and dust are drawn ever more closely into a tight ball by the effects of gravity. This releases enormous amounts of heat. Eventually it becomes hot enough to shine.

1

2

2–3 During much of its life a star burns hydrogen gas and shines brightly and little change appears to happen for billions of years.

3

Star begins to grow

4–7 Eventually the hydrogen fuel is used up and only helium is left to burn. As helium burns at much higher temperatures than hydrogen, the star gets brighter. At the same time the outer part of the star begins to expand again, forming a red giant star.

4

Black holes
Very large stars of a certain size never blow up to form supernovae but collapse more gently, getting smaller and smaller, and denser and denser and their gravity becoming stronger and stronger.

Nobody knows what these bodies look like because the pull of gravity is so great no light ever leaves them. They are the most mysterious features of the universe and are called black holes.

5

6

A supernova is a red giant that explodes. It suddenly increases in brightness by a factor of many billions, but even within a few weeks it begins to fade. The Crab Nebula (shown in this picture and some 8000 light years away) consists of material ejected by the supernova of 1054.

A supernova may radiate more energy in a few days than the Sun does in 100 million years. The stellar remnant left behind after the explosion is a star only a few kilometres in diameter but with an enormously high density.

8–11 Eventually the star literally blows apart and produces the spectacular 'fireworks' in space called a supernova. The remnant star then contracts as a neutron star or white dwarf, spinning quickly and sending out pulses of radio waves like a galactic beacon. This is why a neutron star is also sometimes called a pulsar. Eventually the neutron star dies, its heat is lost and it ceases to shine. Although it still exists in the galaxy, it can no longer be seen and it is called a black dwarf.

Black dwarf **11**

White dwarf
(neutron star, pulsar) **10**

9

Nebula

Red giant

8

7

New words

atmosphere

the layers of gases that surround the Earth. The lowest layer is made up mainly of nitrogen and oxygen and also contains carbon dioxide and water vapour. The air thins out rapidly away from the Earth's surface but it still has an important effect on our world by trapping harmful ultra-violet radiation from the Sun

atom

an atom is the smallest possible piece of a substance, the basic building block of all materials. The entire Universe is made up of just 92 stable elements

axis (axes)

an axis is an imaginary 'spindle' about which something rotates. The Earth, like every other body, spins in space around an imaginary spindle that goes through the North and South Poles

Big Bang

the theory known as the Big Bang assumes that the Universe started from a single point, 15 – 30 billion years ago, and that since this first time everything has been travelling outwards, like the pieces thrown out by some immense explosion

convection

this is the process whereby liquids turn over and over when heated from below. Convection is thought to happen in the Earth's mantle, and it is responsible for the movement of the continents

gravity

this is the force that accompanies every piece of matter in the Universe. The gravity force varies with the mass (size) of the body, which is why most Suns (which are far bigger than planets) produce the most powerful gravitational forces. The only exception to this is a collapsing star, which often has a small size but produces an enormous gravitational force

Greenhouse Effect

the warming of the atmosphere produced by burning fossil fuels is called the Greenhouse Effect. This is because the effect of pollution gases on our air is to trap heat from the Sun, with the same effect as the way that heat builds up inside a greenhouse on a sunny day

Ice Age

this is the time, beginning about a million years ago, when the Earth's climate cooled down and ice sheets spread across large areas of the continents

kilowatt (kW)

this is a unit of power. A one bar electric fire produces an output of about 1 kW of heat per second

mantle

the processes that go on inside planets normally produce several different layers. The inner layer is called the core, the outer layer is called the crust. The layer between the core and the crust is called the mantle. Not much is known about the mantles of the other planets in the Solar System, but the Earth's mantle is thought to be made of materials rather like the basalt lava that makes up much of the rocks on the ocean floors

meteorite

Small pieces of rock travelling through space are called meteoroids. They are smaller than asteroids but bigger than dust.

Meteoroids are called meteors or shooting stars if they burn up and create a trail of light as they fall through the Earth's atmosphere.

Some meteoroids reach the Earth's surface before they burn up entirely, and the rocky body that creates a huge crater on impact is called a meteorite

nuclear reaction

nuclear reactions take place when energy is given out by atoms in a special way. Enormous temperatures and pressures may be needed to make nuclear reactions, but when they occur, they release very large amounts of energy. Nuclear reactions are continually taking place inside the Sun

orbit

the path that one body takes as it goes round a larger body. The Moon orbits the Earth in a path that is almost circular; the Earth and Moon together orbit the Sun in a path that is much more oval (called elliptical)

photon

this is the smallest possible 'packet' of light. Photons are given out when special changes, such as great heating, take place in atoms. A stream of photons is seen as a beam of light

Solar System

this is the name given to the group of planets and other bodies that orbit the Sun. Two opposing forces hold all the planets in their orbits. Imagine a ball being whirled around your head on a string, the whirling force which would send the ball far away if you let go of the string is due to the speed of the planets; the string that holds the ball in place is the force of gravity produced by the Sun. There are nine planets, at least 54 Moons, more than 1,000 comets, and countless asteroids and meteoroids, together with a background of dust

Universe

this is the name given to the entirety of everything that we know about. It includes the Solar System, the Galaxy and all other galaxies beyond the reach of our most powerful telescopes

Index